TWELFTH EDITION

The Education Act, 1944

Provisions, Regulations, Circulars, Later Acts

H. C. Dent

 University of London Press Ltd

SBN 340 08718 8

First published 1944
Twelfth edition copyright © H. C. Dent 1968

University of London Press Ltd
St Paul's House, Warwick Lane, London EC4

Hazell Watson & Viney Ltd, Aylesbury, Bucks

62'2 P

HUB

THE EDUCATION ACT, 1944

Contents

Introduction

THE Education Act, 1944, first of a series of major measures of social reconstruction, became law on 3 August of that year. The Bill was piloted through Parliament by Mr R. A. (now Lord) Butler, who was then President of the Board of Education, and the Act is frequently referred to as the 'Butler Act'. Not without reason, for Mr Butler was largely responsible for both the contents of the Bill and its remarkably smooth passage through Parliament.

It is a very great Act, which makes—and, in fact, has made—possible as important and substantial an advance in public education as this country has ever known. But in itself 'legislation can do little more than prepare the way for reform', as Mr Butler's White Paper, *Educational Reconstruction* (July 1943) rightly warned. The value of an Act of Parliament depends upon how fully it is put into operation and how well it is administered; and this in turn depends very largely upon the public approval and support that the measure commands.

No one will imagine that it is either a quick or an easy matter to bring so massive an Education Act fully into operation. Given the best will in the world and the most favourable circumstances the task would still be long, difficult and costly. It is the country's misfortune that it has to be carried out during a period of economic and social dislocation and simultaneously with other large schemes of social welfare. After 23 years there are still important Sections of the Act not implemented; yet nothing less than complete implementation will suffice to satisfy the nation's needs.

Those who have to administer the Act need all possible help from the general public. This can only be given if every citizen—man and woman—knows what is in the Act, what opportunities it offers, and what difficulties and problems its administration presents.

This book is intended to help teachers, parents, students, and members of the general public to play a part in making this great Education Act a complete success. In it I outline, as simply as may be, the main provisions of the Act, and comment briefly upon some of its possibilities and some of the difficulties it presents. I include also summaries of the 'amending' Acts that have altered particular points in the 'principal' Act: the Education Act, 1946, the Education (Miscellaneous Provisions) Act, 1948, the Education (Miscellaneous Provisions) Act, 1953, and the Education Acts of 1959, 1962, 1964, and 1967. None of these alters the main structure of the 1944 Act. The Remuneration of Teachers Act, 1965, does, however, make an important change in the machinery for determining teachers' salaries.

This edition has also been revised to include notes on Regulations and Circulars issued up to 30 September 1967.

The Education Act, 1944, lays unprecedented obligations upon both the public authorities and the private citizen. Its full implementation may make all the difference between a happy and glorious future for our country and an unhappy and inglorious one. To make it a real success, the wholehearted co-operation of every citizen is required.

Summary of Contents

THE Act is arranged in 5 Parts containing 122 Sections, or Clauses as they are often called, and 9 Schedules. These latter deal in detail with matters arising out of various clauses.

Part I (Sections 1–5) deals with the Central Administration: the duties of the Minister; his officers, and the Advisory Councils for England and Wales.

Part II (Sections 6–69) deals with the Statutory System of Education, that is, the educational services provided or aided out of public funds and available to the general public; primary, secondary, and further education (formal and informal, including the Service of Youth); and the various services ancillary to these, such as the School Health Service and the provision of milk and meals at school.

Part III (Sections 70–75) deals with independent, that is private, schools.

Part IV (Sections 76–107) contains a variety of miscellaneous provisions, dealing with such matters as the inspection of schools, the powers of the Minister and the local authorities to grant scholarships, the rights of parents, and the financial arrangements between the Ministry, the local authorities, and the voluntary bodies co-operating in the educational services.

Part V (Sections 108–122) deals mainly with bringing the Act into operation, and includes an 'interpretation' clause defining the more important terms used in the Act.

The schedules deal with such matters as the composition and functions of local education authorities and other bodies, and the amendment and repeal of previous Acts.

Parts I and V came into operation the day the Act received the Royal Assent, Parts II and IV on 1 April 1945.[1] Part III came into operation on 30 September 1957.

In the following pages I deal with the Parts and Sections as

[1] Except that the raising of the compulsory school age to 15 was postponed to 1 April 1947.

they are arranged in the Act, except that various financial and supplementary provisions are noted in connection with previous sections to which they refer.

NOTE.—By Order in Council (The Secretary of State for Education and Science Order, 1964) all the functions of the Minister of Education were on 1 April 1964 transferred to the Secretary of State for Education and Science, and the Ministry of Education became a part of the Department of Education and Science.

The Department is concerned with university education and civil science throughout Great Britain, but with primary, secondary and further education in England and Wales only. In 1967 there were in the Department, as assistants to the Secretary of State, three Ministers of State. Each had defined responsibilities, but ultimate responsibility lies always with the Secretary of State.

In this book the term 'Minister' is almost everywhere retained as shorter and less cumbrous—and even a Secretary of State is a Minister of the Crown!

PART ONE

Central Administration

FROM 1900, when the Board of Education was established, until 1944 the Minister was styled the President of the Board of Education (though in fact the Board never met), and his responsibility to Parliament and the public was 'the superintendence of certain matters relating to education in England and Wales'.

Under the 1944 Act his title became that of Minister, and his duty to—

promote the education of the people of England and Wales and the progressive development of institutions devoted to that purpose, and to secure the effective execution by local authorities, under his control and direction, of the national policy for providing a varied and comprehensive educational service in every area. (Section 1.)

This section clearly places very large powers in the hands of the Minister. During the passage of the Bill fears were expressed, both in Parliament and outside, that they were too large, that in effect they made the Minister a dictator; and an amendment was moved in the House of Commons to omit the words 'under his control and direction'. Mr Butler resisted this, and was supported by the House. Sir Percy Harris, the leader of the Liberal Party, voiced the general feeling when he said that if the Act was to work it was vital that the Minister 'should be armed with full power and authority to force education authorities up to one common level'; and Mr Butler was warmly applauded when he declared that he intended the central authority to 'lead boldly and not follow timidly'—without, he was at pains to emphasize, either destroying or diminishing the spirit of partnership in which it had always worked with the local authorities.

There is a very strong case for effective central direction and control. A national service must be nationally directed. It was previously a major defect in English educational administration

that local authorities could with impunity be laggard or reaction-
ary in their provision, thus denying children (and adults) in their
areas opportunities available in the areas of enlightened and progressive authorities, because the President of the Board of Education had no statutory power to compel such backward authorities
to raise their standards.

Yet there is substance in the fear that such large powers as the
Act gives to the Minister could open the door to an educational
dictatorship. This fear need never be realized, provided Parliament and the public are alive to their responsibilities. The Minister
is answerable for his actions and those of his department to Parliament, to which he must render an annual report 'giving an account
of the exercise and performance of the powers and duties conferred
and imposed upon him by this Act' (Section 5). Any Regulation
he makes must be laid before Parliament, and either House has
power to annul it (Section 112). He can be publicly questioned by
any member of the House of Commons[1] on any day the House is
sitting (and privately by any citizen at any time) concerning any
action of his own, of any of his officers, or of any person engaged
in the statutory service of public education. It is important to remember in this connection that every citizen has the right (and the
duty) to bring to the notice of his member of Parliament any
matter into which he feels inquiry ought to be made.

A further check is imposed upon the Minister by Section 4,
which provides for two Central Advisory Councils for Education,
one for England and one for Wales and Monmouthshire. The
duty of these councils is—

to advise the Minister upon such matters connected with educational
theory and practice *as they think fit*, and upon any questions referred to
them by him.

The vitally important words in this charge are those which I
have italicized. There was previously as part of the machinery of
the Board of Education a Consultative Committee to which the
President could, and did, refer matters for detailed inquiry and
report; and some exceedingly valuable reports resulted from the
investigations of this committee.[2] But it had no power to conduct

[1] The House of Lords has no 'question time'.
[2] Notably the 'Hadow' Report on *The Education of the Adolescent* (1926),
as a result of which the reorganization of the public elementary school into
primary and post-primary divisions was undertaken.

inquiries on its own initiative. The councils have this power, and provided they are composed of men and women of independent mind, with the courage of their convictions, they can be not only of the greatest assistance to the Minister but also a powerful deterrent to arbitrary or irresponsible action on his part, despite the fact that their functions are limited to educational theory and practice, and do not extend to administration.

It is true, too, that the Minister himself appoints the chairmen, members, and secretaries of the councils, and by Regulations[1] determines for how long they shall serve. This would seem to take away much of their value as a check upon him. But against this has to be set the fact that he must include in his annual report to Parliament an account 'of the composition and proceedings' of the councils (Section 5).

A prolonged debate took place in the House of Commons concerning the composition of these councils. Various members desired to see direct representation of specific interests—industry, agriculture, adult education, technical education, for example. Mr Butler resisted all such proposals, saying that he wanted the councils to be as broadly representative of the national life as possible. Despite strong pressure, he stuck to the purposed vagueness of Section 4, which merely requires that each council shall include persons with experience of the statutory system of education and persons with experience of other educational institutions. The House of Lords inserted a proviso that as to one-third of the members of the councils the Minister must consult beforehand the President of the Board of Trade and the Minister of Agriculture, but happily the Commons rejected this singularly ill-conceived proposal.

Mr Butler defined the intended function of the councils very clearly. They were not to concern themselves with administration, but to—

pay some attention to what is taught in the schools and . . . to all the most modern and up-to-date methods, and by reviewing the position continually consider the whole question of what may be taught to the children. (*Hansard*, 8 February 1944, Vol. 396, No. 26, col. 1707.)

The rest of Part I of the Act calls for little comment. Section 1 (3) empowers the Minister to appoint a Parliamentary Secretary,

[1] See *Central Advisory Councils for Education Regulations, 1945 and 1951.* (S.R. and O., 1945, No. 152, and 1951, No. 1742.)

and 'such other secretaries, officers, and servants as the Minister may, with the consent of the Treasury, determine'. The statutory provision here remains unchanged. Sections 2 and 3 deal with the transfer of property and functions to the Minister and the authentication of documents issued by him.

PART TWO

The Statutory System of Education

I Local Administration

SECTION 6 provoked more discussion in the House of Commons than any other. It lays down that—

subject to the provisions of Part I of the First Schedule to this Act, the local education authority for each county shall be the council of the county, and the local education authority for each county borough shall be the council of the county borough.

This effected something of a revolution in the local administration of education, for it meant that 169 of the then existing 315 local education authorities ceased to exist on 1 April 1945, when Part II of the Act came into operation. Hence the excitement.

Why should such a drastic change have been thought necessary? For the answer one must go back to the Education Act of 1902. This set up the machinery of local administration which was in 1944 so strikingly modified. It made the county councils and the county borough councils local education authorities for all forms of public education. (These authorities, because their powers and duties were specified in Part II of the 1902 Act, became known as 'Part II Authorities'.) It also made municipal boroughs with a population exceeding 10,000 at the 1901 census and urban district councils with a population exceeding 20,000 (also in 1901) local education authorities *for elementary education only* within their areas. These were the 'Part III Authorities'. It was the Part III Authorities which were abolished by the 1944 Act.

As they stood, they were bound to be. Under Section 7 of the Act the category 'elementary' disappeared from the English educational system, and consequently local education authorities for elementary education only had to disappear also. But that did not mean, said the champions of the Part III Authorities, that these authorities should cease to exist altogether. No: raise their status, not extinguish them. Make them 'all-purpose' education authorities, like the county councils and the county borough councils. They had been exercising educational functions for over forty years, and in many cases doing so extremely well. Among their ranks were some of the most progressive and efficient education authorities in the county—notably more so than many counties. Moreover, some of them, being ancient boroughs, had been exercising other local government functions for centuries, while some had grown so rapidly since 1902 that they were in 1944 larger in population and wealthier than some of the counties and county boroughs.

But there were weak links in this apparently strong case. The majority of the Part III Authorities, it had to be admitted, were too small, and lacked the necessary financial resources, for so comprehensive an educational service as the Act projected. There were urban districts without educational powers that were far larger and wealthier. To pick and choose an entirely new set of authorities would take time—lots of time; and Mr Butler wanted his Act in operation quickly. So, too, he knew, did an overwhelming majority of the people of England and Wales. There was no time for a comprehensive inquiry into the structure of local government.

Still, something had clearly to be conceded to the Part IIIs. A compromise had to be arranged. That compromise is to be found in the first Schedule to the Act.

Part I of this Schedule provides that the Minister may constitute a 'joint education board'[1] for the areas of two or more counties or county boroughs judged too small or poor to carry by themselves the full burden of a comprehensive education service.

Part III of the Schedule provides that the areas of counties (the provision does not apply to county boroughs) may be partitioned 'into such divisions as may be conducive to efficient and convenient administration', and that in these bodies of persons to be known as 'divisional executives' shall be constituted to exercise

[1] One joint board, for the Soke of Peterborough and the City of Peterborough, was set up.

on behalf of the authority 'such functions relating to primary and secondary education[1] as may be so specified'. The only powers which the authority may not delegate are those of borrowing money and raising a rate.

Schemes of divisional administration are made by the local education authority,[2] but the Act provided that the council of any borough or urban district could, before 1 October 1944, lodge a claim to 'be excepted from any scheme of divisional administration to be made by a local education authority'. If the population of the borough or urban district was in 1939 not less than 60,000, or its elementary school population not less than 7,000, the Minister had to allow the claim. In other cases he consulted with the local education authority and any other councils concerned, and allowed the claim if he considered that special circumstances justified it. The council of an 'excepted district' has the right to make (after consultation with the local education authority) its own scheme of divisional administration.[3]

Opinions have always varied about the value of this somewhat intricate arrangement, and from time to time proposals have been made to abolish divisional executives. The truth appears to be that where there has been co-operation in a spirit of goodwill between the authority and the executives, as there has been in many areas, it has proved helpful, and has, as Mr Butler hoped, created 'something new and valuable in the sphere of local government'. But there have been many complaints that the system of divisional administration is unduly expensive, creates delays, and diminishes the powers and responsibilities of managers and governors of schools.

The matter is part of the larger question of the future of local government. This question intimately affects public education, which is by far the largest and most costly local authority function. Most people who work in or have studied educational administration in England and Wales would be very reluctant to see local authorities playing a less important part in it. But, apart

[1] And, in certain circumstances, further education. See Education Act, 1946, Second Schedule, Part I.

[2] See Ministry of Education Circular 5, *Schemes of Divisional Administration*, for the general principles on which such schemes are based.

[3] At 1 October 1967 there were 173 divisional executives, of which 33 were excepted districts. There can be no further applications for Excepted District Status until 1969.

from considerations of size, population, and financial resources, it has to be remembered that effective local administration depends upon there being always a sufficient number of able men and women willing to serve education on local councils and committees.

II   *The System Recast*

Section 7 is the most important in the Act. It entirely recast the structure of the statutory system of public education. Previously this was organized in two parts: elementary and higher education, the latter including all forms of education other than elementary. As secondary education began at 11+ and junior technical at 12 or 13, while elementary continued compulsorily until 14, these parts overlapped. But as maintained secondary schools were available for only about 20 per cent. of the children eligible by age, and junior technical schools for under one per cent., there was a grave inadequacy of educational opportunity for young adolescents. For some 80 per cent. of the children attending State schools (who made up over 90 per cent. of all children) an elementary education only was available.

That unhappy state of affairs was ended by the 1944 Act. Section 7 says that—

The statutory system of public education shall be organized in three progressive stages to be known as primary education, secondary education, and further education;

and that—

it shall be the duty of the local education authority for every area, so far as their powers extend, to contribute towards the spiritual, moral, mental, and physical development of the community by securing that efficient education throughout those stages shall be available to meet the needs of the population of their area.

Previously, it was the *duty* of the local authorities to provide elementary education only, though Part II authorities had *powers* to provide or aid the provision of secondary and other higher education. How adequately those powers were exercised depended upon the attitude towards education of a local authority or upon the financial resources at their command; and, consequently, the provision of higher education was extremely unequal—and very rarely sufficient. It is now the statutory duty of every local education authority to make available throughout their area efficient facilities for primary and secondary education for every boy and girl, and for further education for every man and woman who desires it. It is the duty of every citizen to see that duty *well* done.

The financial implications of this will be discussed later. Meanwhile, it is to be noted that Section 8 goes into considerable detail concerning the provision of primary and secondary education. The local authority must see that in their area there are sufficient schools for providing (*a*) primary education, which is defined as 'full-time education suitable to the requirements of junior pupils' (i.e. pupils under 12 years of age), and (*b*) secondary education, that is, 'full-time education suitable to the needs of senior pupils' (i.e. over 12 but under 19).[1]

In amplification of the above there comes the following glorious passage, which should be hung up in the meeting-room of every local education committee and learned by heart by every citizen:

and the schools available for an area shall not be deemed to be sufficient unless they are sufficient in number, character, and equipment to afford for all pupils opportunities for education offering such variety of instruction and training as may be desirable in view of their different ages, abilities, and aptitudes, and of the different periods for which they may be expected to remain at school, including practical instruction and training appropriate to their respective needs.

A volume of commentary might be written on that passage, but it must suffice to say here that properly interpreted it will mean full and appropriate educational opportunity for every boy and girl throughout the period of compulsory schooling, and, if desired, beyond it to age 19.

No one could pretend that it is easy to achieve this ideal. Many reasons have made it extremely difficult. At the time of the passing of the Act the country's school buildings, especially the elementary school buildings, were on the whole out-of-date and

---

[1] These definitions were modified in 1948. See pages 108–9.

much below what present-day standards[1] demand. Many were squalid, and not a few insanitary. It was estimated even before the war by a competent authority[2] that four out of every five elementary schools ought to be rebuilt. During the war over 5,000 schools —or accommodation for upwards of 300,000 pupils—were destroyed or seriously damaged by enemy action. The raising of the school age to 15 increased the school population by 350,000. A steep and continuing rise in the birth-rate has increased the numbers of children in school by one-third. The number of children staying voluntarily at school beyond the age of 15 grows larger year by year. The raising of the school leaving age to 16 in 1970 will require still more accommodation.

A very large school building programme, still proceeding, had produced over 7,500 new schools by the end of 1966. A similarly sustained effort had increased five-fold the pre-war output of trained teachers. But these programmes, splendid in themselves, have only barely kept pace with the increase in the number of pupils—from 5,100,000 in 1946 to about 8,000,000 in 1967. And there is a third task, the remaking of the education given in schools to match up to the requirements of the Act. No praise can be too high for much of the experimental work that has been done by teachers, local authorities, and research workers since 1945. This has literally transformed the life and spirit of numerous schools, making them altogether happier and more purposeful places. Yet, even so, much more remains to be done before the ideal of Section 8, particularly that part which demands—

such variety of training and instruction as may be desirable in view of their different ages, abilities, and aptitudes,

will be fully realized.

No mention of the size of classes will be found in the Act. Determined attempts were made in Parliament to include a limiting figure. The Government's reply was that this was a matter for administration, not legislation. Mr (later Lord) Chuter Ede,

[1] For the minimum standards originally required under the 1944 Act, see *Regulations prescribing Standards for School Premises, 1945* (S.R. and O., 1945, No. 345). Regulations made in 1951, 1954 and 1959 reduced the requirements somewhat and made them less rigid.

[2] The late Dr F. H. Spencer, a former Chief Inspector to the London County Council, in *Education for the People* (Routledge).

Parliamentary Secretary to the Board of Education, said on 15 February 1944:

By insisting that under Regulations the size of classes shall be continually reduced ... we shall be able to make progress a great deal more quickly than in inserting something in the Bill which will from time to time require all the machinery of an Act of Parliament to alter. (*Hansard*, Vol. 397, No. 30, cols. 128–9.)

The wisdom of this argument is, in my opinion, irreproachable. But it must be backed by determined and sustained action; there is no educational reform more sorely needed than the abolition of over-large classes, which make good teaching exacting if not impossible. As the White Paper said, such classes mean not education but mass production. Unhappily, the Regulations obtaining in 1967[1] still allowed up to 40 pupils in primary school classes. Reduction was long ago promised 'directly the necessary increase in the supply of teachers and school accommodation makes it reasonably possible'. That promise has not yet been fulfilled.

Section 8 goes on to instruct local education authorities, when making their provision of schools, to have particular regard to four points:

1   Separate schools for primary and secondary education.
2   The needs of children under 5.
3   The needs of children suffering from 'any disability of mind or body'.
4   The 'expediency of securing the provision of boarding accommodation, either in boarding schools or otherwise, for pupils for whom education as boarders is considered by their parents and by the authority to be desirable'.

I have quoted the last direction in full, because this is the first occasion in our educational history that local education authorities have been statutorily enjoined to set up boarding schools. The wisdom of the other directions is self-evident.

Section 9 gives the local education authorities the necessary powers to establish and maintain and to assist primary and secondary schools, outside as well as inside their areas; and deals with nomenclature. Maintained schools (except nursery and special schools) if established by the authority are termed 'county schools',

[1] See *The Schools Regulations, 1959.*

if by other bodies 'voluntary schools'. Primary schools used mainly
to provide education for children between 2 and 5 are 'nursery
schools'. Schools especially organized for the purpose of providing
special educational treatment for handicapped children are 'special
schools'.

Section 10 lays it down that—

The Minister shall make regulations[1] prescribing the standards to
which the premises of schools maintained by local education authorities are to conform;

and that subject to exceptions for special circumstances the local
authorities must see to it that the premises of all their maintained
schools conform to the prescribed standards. This is a most important section. It should be related to the ideal set out in Section 8,
and public opinion should not be satisfied unless and until the
school premises in every area are such as to make the realization of
that ideal possible. The Regulations issued in 1945—the first of
their kind ever made—were admirable, and it is unfortunate that
the vast size of the school building programme has compelled
some economies which must be regretted.

It must be added that most of the schools built under the
strict post-war cost limits compare favourably with those of any
other country. The greatest credit is due to the Ministry of
Education, the local education authorities, and their architects for
having regarded economy, not as a reason for poorer quality, but
as a spur to greater efficiency.

Section 11 was (and is) of the utmost importance. It laid down
that within a year of the coming into operation of Part II of the
Act (that is, within a year of 1 April 1945) every local education
authority had to prepare and submit to the Minister a 'development plan' showing what the authority proposed to do to secure
that there should be 'sufficient' (remember Section 8) primary and
secondary schools in their area; and how they proposed to do it.
These plans are the foundation upon which has been built the
massive post-war expansion and improvement of primary and
secondary schools.

Most of the local authorities found the time allowed too
short. In March 1946 the Minister, in Circular 90, granted them

[1] See page 14.

leave to apply for an extension of up to three months, or longer if they could show special cause. Several authorities, including the London County Council, at once applied for an extension of one year, and many others found they could not complete the task in less time. By the end of 1951, almost all the local education authorities had submitted complete plans.

When the Minister has approved a development plan, he issues a 'local education order' (Section 12), which defines the 'duty of the authority with respect to the measures to be taken'. If the local authority object to the order and 'inform the Minister that they are aggrieved', then it must be laid before Parliament, and either House may within 40 days annul it. The same applies to any amendment of an order. An amendment may be made by the Minister only after he has given notice to the authority and any schools concerned; and they have two months in which to submit objections.

Sections 13 and 14 deal with the establishment and discontinuance of schools, their purpose being to provide that there shall be adequate consultation before so important a step is taken. Public notice must be given of any such proposal, which must be submitted to the Minister; and school managers or governors or 'any ten or more local government electors for the area' have two months[1] in which to submit objections. The importance of these sections was vividly illustrated by the Enfield court cases in 1967.

Two years' notice must be given of the proposed discontinuance of a voluntary school, and except by leave of the Minister it may not be given at all if he or the local authority have incurred expenditure (except for repairs) on the establishment or alteration of the school. If notice has been given, and the managers or governors cannot carry on the school during the interim period, the local authority can assume complete control.

III Dual Control

The compromise on the 'Dual Control' of schools is one of the outstanding triumphs of the Act: not because it satisfies everybody (in fact, it completely satisfies no one), but because it is a

---

[1] Originally three months; reduced to two by the Education (Miscellaneous Provisions) Act, 1953, Section 16.

compromise which all parties concerned agreed to accept. This had never happened before, and it is the more remarkable in that, as under the Act all post-primary schools became secondary, Dual Control was for the first time extended into the field of secondary education.

Section 15 names the three categories of voluntary schools: *controlled, aided,* and *special agreement,* and specifies the financial obligations of their managers or governors.

The managers or governors of a 'controlled school' do not have to finance any expenditure, capital or current, on the school. This is done by the local education authority.

The managers or governors of an 'aided school' or a 'special agreement school' are responsible for—

the expenses of discharging any liability incurred by them or on their behalf or by or on behalf of any former managers or governors of the school or any trustees thereof in connection with the provision of premises or equipment for the purposes of the school, any expenses incurred in effecting such alterations to the school buildings as may be required by the local education authority for the purpose of securing that the school buildings should conform to the prescribed standards, and any expenses incurred in effecting repairs to the school building, except repairs to the interior of the school buildings, or resulting from use of the buildings by the local education authority for purposes other than those of the school.[1]

The above arrangement looks (and is) complicated.[2] I give it in full, for three reasons: first, because the sharing of the financial responsibility for a voluntary school as between the local authority and the school managers or governors has been a matter of controversy ever since sharing was first mooted; second, because there is much misunderstanding as to what exactly the respective obligations are; and thirdly, because for the first time the voluntary schools were offered a choice of alternatives, carrying different privileges and obligations. I want therefore to make the position of voluntary schools under the Act as clear as is possible in a brief summary. The managers or governors of a controlled school have no financial obligations whatsoever; the entire responsibility falls

---

[1] See Section 15 (3) (a) and (b), as amended by the Education Act, 1946.

[2] For detailed discussion of the intricacies involved see *County and Voluntary Schools,* by Sir William Alexander and F. Barraclough (Councils and Education Press), 4th edition, 1967.

upon the local education authority. The managers or governors of an aided school or a special agreement school are responsible for the capital expenditure on alterations required by the local authority to keep the premises up to standard, and for expenditure on repairs to the exterior of the buildings. The local education authority is responsible for all running costs, including teachers' salaries, for repairs to the interior of the building, to the playground and playing-fields, and for the erection and maintenance of buildings used exclusively for the school health and meals services.

But while the managers or governors of an aided or special agreement school are *responsible* for certain specified categories of expenditure, they do not have to find all the money to meet these expenses. Up to 1959 they had to find half.[1] Section 102 (as amended by the Education Act, 1946) laid down that—

The Minister shall pay to the managers or governors of every aided school and of every special agreement school maintenance contributions equal to one-half of any sums expended by them in carrying out their obligations under paragraph (*a*) of sub-section (3) of Section 15 on this Act in respect of alterations and repairs to the school buildings:

Provided that no maintenance contribution shall be payable under this section in respect of any expenditure incurred by the managers or governors of a special agreement school in the execution of which provision is made by the special agreement relating to the school.

The 'special agreement school' was a product of the Education Act of 1936. In order to hasten on the reorganization of the elementary school system, local education authorities were empowered to make 'special agreements' with managers for the establishment, or alteration of the premises, of senior elementary schools under which grants of public money of not less than one-half or more than three-quarters of the cost of executing the proposals might be made. Five hundred and nineteen agreements were entered into (289 being put up by managers of Roman Catholic schools), but owing to the war only 37 of the projects materialized. The Third Schedule of the 1944 Act provides that the unfulfilled agreements may be revived, with such revisions as may be desir-

[1] The Education Act, 1959, raised the grant payable to 75 per cent., the Education Act, 1967, to 80 per cent.

able. All proposals have to be made within six months of the date upon which the local education order for the area comes into force,[1] and all agreements have to be approved by the Minister.

IV   Religious Education

What is the other side of the bargain between the Government and the voluntary schools? It covers three points: the management or government of the schools, the religious instruction given in them, and the appointment and dismissal of teachers.

With the first of these points—the management or government of schools—I will deal later in a separate section, since this matter raises also questions of general interest to all schools.

Before coming to the agreement about religious instruction it should be noted first that (Section 23) the secular instruction in all county schools and all voluntary schools except aided secondary schools is under the control of the local education authority.[2] In an aided secondary school it is under the control of the governors. As regards religious education in general, it is laid down in Section 25 that—

the school day in every county school and in every voluntary school shall begin with collective worship on the part of all pupils in attendance,

and that—

religious instruction shall be given in every county school and in every voluntary school.

This was a new departure in our educational legislation. Though religious instruction and daily collective acts of worship had for long previously been virtually universal in the schools, they had never been made statutory obligations. The teachers' organizations protested strongly against what seemed to them an unnecessary and humiliating compulsion; and they received very considerable public and Parliamentary support. The Government's decision to enforce compulsion had behind it a long history which there is

---

[1] 'or such extended period as the Minister may in any particular case allow'.

[2] Except 'in so far as may be otherwise provided by the rules of management or articles of government for the school'.

no space to discuss here. The following reason for it was given during the Parliamentary debate by Mr Chuter Ede:

There is, I think, a general recognition that even if parents themselves have in the course of life encountered difficulties that have led them into doubts and hesitations, they do desire that their children shall have a grounding in the principles of the Christian faith as it ought to be practised in this country. (*Hansard*, 10 March 1944, Vol. 397, No. 45, col. 2425.)

Consequently, runs the argument, there should be no doubt that this grounding will everywhere be given, and the only way to ensure this is to make it a statutory obligation.

The traditional freedom of the parent in respect of religious education has, of course, been preserved. Section 25 lays down that—

It shall not be required, as a condition of any pupil attending any county or voluntary school, that he shall attend or abstain from attending any Sunday school or any place of religious worship;

and that—

If the parent of any pupil in attendance at any county school or any voluntary school requests that he be wholly or partly excused from attendance at religious worship in the school, or from attendance at religious instruction in the school, or from attendance at both religious worship and religious instruction in the school, then, until the request is withdrawn, the pupil shall be excused such attendance accordingly.

Moreover, provided it will not interfere with the pupil's attendance except at the beginning or end of a school session,[1] a pupil may be withdrawn from school to receive such particular religious instruction as his parents desire (Section 25). This applies to boarding as well as day schools.

These provisions lead up to those concerning the nature of the religious worship and instruction in county, controlled, aided, and special agreement schools respectively.

By Section 26 the collective worship in a county school 'shall not . . . be distinctive of any particular religious denomination', and the religious instruction shall be 'in accordance with an agreed syllabus[2] adopted for the school . . . and shall not include any

[1] A 'session' is a morning or afternoon meeting.

[2] The Fifth Schedule provides for the convening by the local authority of a representative conference of interested bodies to prepare an agreed syllabus. See page 63.

catechism or formulary which is distinctive of any particular religious denomination'.

By Section 27 the religious instruction in a controlled school shall be 'in accordance with an agreed syllabus adopted for the school', but if the parents of any pupils in attendance request that they receive religious instruction in accordance with the provisions of the trust deed or the previous practice at the school, then arrangements are to be made for such instruction to be given 'during not more than two periods in each week'. In short, controlled schools are allowed to give denominational religious instruction twice a week.

Provided the teaching staff of the school exceeds two, up to one-fifth of the staff are to be 'selected for their fitness and competence to give such religious instruction'. These are called 'reserved teachers' (Section 27). A head teacher may not be counted as a reserved teacher.

In aided and special agreement schools the religious instruction—

shall be under the control of the managers or governors of the school, and shall be in accordance with any provisions of the trust deed relating to the school, or, where provision for that purpose is not made by such a deed, in accordance with the practice observed in the school before it became a voluntary school (Section 28).

In other words, in an aided or special agreement school all the religious instruction may be (and doubtless will be) denominational instruction.

In the case of all the categories of schools, except the county primary school, however, provision is made (within certain defined limits) for meeting the wishes of parents who desire a different form of religious instruction from that given to the majority of pupils. In specified instances, accommodation must be provided for the giving of such special instruction on the school premises.

V   School Governance

If a school is to have a life of its own, and not become merely a unit in a system, it is essential that it shall be the particular care of a body of people charged with looking after its interests. It has always been the practice in England and Wales to have such a body; but unfortunately, owing to the different histories of the elementary and secondary school systems, two different systems of school governance evolved: of *management* for elementary schools, and of *government* for secondary schools. The 1944 Act, to the disappointment of many people, did not abolish this distinction. It retained management for primary schools and government for secondary schools. The reason, said Mr Chuter Ede, was that—

The machinery that now exists in local government for creating governing bodies is the kind of machinery which it is necessary to provide for the new and wider secondary schools of the future. But, with regard to the primary school, I do not think they want the terrific machinery that the English governing body really is. (*Hansard*, 9 March 1944, Vol. 397, No. 44, col. 2243.)

The following outline of the machinery may help the reader to make up his mind whether that opinion is justified.

In the first place—

For every county school and for every voluntary school there shall be an instrument providing for the constitution of the body of managers or governors of the school in accordance with the provisions of this Act (Section 17).

In the case of a primary school this is to be called an 'instrument of management', of a secondary school an 'instrument of government'.

Every primary school is to be conducted in accordance with 'rules of management', every secondary school in accordance with 'articles of government'. The 'rules of management' are to be made by the local education authority, as are also the 'articles of government' for a county secondary school, though these latter must be approved by the Minister. The 'articles of government' for a voluntary secondary school are to be made by an order of the Minister (Section 17), which means in effect that the governors submit a scheme for approval. Before making an order the Minister must give the local authority and any other people or bodies concerned an opportunity to make representations about it.

It will be seen from the foregoing that the more independent tradition of the secondary school has secured it rather more freedom than the primary school. The local education authority has a completely free hand in framing rules of management, but far from it with articles of government.

Section 18 provides, first, that if a county primary school serves an area in which there is a minor authority (i.e. the council of a non-county borough, urban district, or parish[1]), that minor authority shall appoint one-third of the managers, the local education authority appointing the other two-thirds; and second, that:

if the school is an aided school or a special agreement school, two-thirds of the managers shall be foundation managers (i.e. appointed by the voluntary body owning the school), and if the school is a controlled school, one-third of the managers shall be foundation managers (Section 18).

(The same conditions apply here concerning the proportion of representatives of the local education authority and the minor authority, but the authorities are limited to sharing the non-foundation managers.)

A body of managers must not be less than six persons (Section 18). This is a valuable advance on previous legislation, which limited the number to six. It does something to narrow the gulf between boards of managers and boards of governors, and makes possible more adequate representation of the interests concerned, including parents and teachers.

There is no limit to the numbers of a governing body of a secondary school; and in practice governing bodies have always been larger than bodies of managers. The governing body of a county school is to be appointed by the local education authority, of a voluntary school by the Minister after consultation with the local education authority. The same proportions of foundation and non-foundation members are to be observed as in the case of primary schools (Section 19).

Section 20 provides that the local education authority may set up a single governing body for any two or more of their maintained schools, whether county or voluntary (though in the latter case only with the consent of the managers or governors of a school concerned). This provision was, and is, resented by many of the older-established secondary schools, which are devoted to the idea of one school one governing body. Clearly, an autocratic local authority could by use of this power gravely diminish the

[1] Or the parish meeting if there is no council.

autonomy of a school. Cases of this are, unhappily, not unknown; hence the apprehension with which schools regard it. On the other hand, the local authorities maintain that without some such arrangement it is impossible to find enough competent men and women who are able to give the time to serve on boards of management or government, and unfortunately this would appear to be true in some areas at least. It should not be; there should be an abundance of citizens ready and able to serve on boards of governors or managers.

VI Appointment and Dismissal of Teachers

It is acknowledged by everybody that the success or failure of any scheme of educational reform depends upon the teachers. The sections dealing with the conditions of service for teachers are therefore of first importance, for unless these are both attractive and fair, sufficient men and women of the necessary quality will not be prepared to enter the profession.

The primary responsibility for securing such conditions is laid upon the Minister. Section 62 lays it down that he shall—

make such arrangements as he considers expedient for securing that there shall be available sufficient facilities for the training of teachers . . . and . . . may give to any local education authority such directions as he thinks necessary requiring them to establish, maintain, or assist any training college or other institution or to provide or assist the provision of any other facilities specified in the direction.[1]

And Section 89 that he shall—

secure that for the purpose of considering the remuneration of teachers there shall be one or more committees approved by him consisting of persons appointed by bodies representing local education authorities and teachers respectively, and it shall be the duty of any such committee to submit to the Minister, whenever they think fit or whenever they may be required by him so to do, such scales of remuneration as they consider suitable; and whenever a scale of remuneration so submitted is approved by the Minister he may by order make such provision as

[1] To gain some idea of what this means in an era of expansion see the Reports of the National Advisory Council on the Training and Supply of Teachers. H.M. Stationery Office.

appears to him to be desirable for the purpose of securing that the remuneration paid by local education authorities to teachers is in accordance therewith.[1]

One essential point in Section 89 must not be overlooked. Since 1919 the remuneration of teachers has been a matter for discussion and agreement by the Burnham Committees, so-called after the first chairman, Viscount Burnham. While their decisions were generally accepted, before 1944 they were not mandatory upon the local authorities, a few of which at times attempted to disregard them. Under the 1944 Act, once the Minister has approved the recommendations of a Burnham Committee (there is one committee for primary and secondary schools and one for further education establishments), all local authorities must pay the agreed salaries.

Appointment and dismissal are naturally subjects of vital concern to the teacher, but, thanks to our tangled educational history, it has often been far from clear where lay the ultimate power to appoint and dismiss. The Act does much to clear up the position.

Section 24 lays it down that in a county school the appointment and dismissal of teachers are both under the control of the local education authority. In a controlled school or a special agreement school appointment is partially under the control of the local education authority. Managers or governors have a say in the appointment of 'reserved teachers', and the rules of management or articles of government may lay down special conditions of appointment; but 'no teacher shall be dismissed except by the authority'. In an aided school the respective functions of the local education authority and the managers or governors are (save in respect of teachers giving religious education) to be regulated by the rules of management or articles of government for the school. A teacher appointed to give denominational religious instruction in an aided school, if he fails to do so 'efficiently and suitably', may be dismissed, *for that reason*, by the managers or governors without the consent of the authority (Section 28).

If the local education authority propose to appoint a 'reserved teacher' to a controlled school, they must obtain the agreement of the managers or governors that he (or she) is a suitable person and

[1] This Section has been substantially altered by the Remuneration of Teachers Act, 1965. See page 115.

professionally competent to give the religious instruction required (Section 27). Should the foundation managers or governors hold that a reserved teacher has failed to give appropriate religious instruction, 'they may require the authority to dismiss him from employment as a reserved teacher in the school' (Section 27). The same conditions obtain in a special agreement school if the agreement provides for the employment of reserved teachers (Section 28).

In an aided school the rules of management or articles of government—

shall make provision for the appointment of the teachers by the managers or governors of the school, for enabling the local education authority to determine the number of teachers to be employed, and for enabling the authority, except for reasons for which the managers or governors are expressly empowered by this Act to dismiss teachers without such consent, to prohibit the dismissal of teachers without the consent of the authority and to require the dismissal of any teacher (Section 24),

and they *may* make provision, by agreement between the local education authority and the managers or governors, or by an order of the Minister if the parties concerned cannot agree—

for enabling the authority to prohibit the appointment, without the consent of the authority, of teachers to be employed for giving secular instruction, and for enabling the authority to give directions as to the educational qualifications of the teachers to be so employed (Section 24).

Section 24 also contains the highly important innovation that—

No woman shall be disqualified for employment as a teacher in any county school or voluntary school or be dismissed from such employment by reason only of marriage.

It is good to see these words at last in an Education Act, though regrettable that it should ever have become necessary to insert them. The country lost much through the previous reluctance of local education authorities to employ married women. How much may be judged by the fact that by 1960 nearly one half (70,000 out of 165,000) of the full-time women teachers in main-

E.A.—3

tained primary and secondary schools were married, as compared
with one in twenty in 1939.

One of the most rooted and long-standing fears of teachers
is that appointment and promotion may be affected by reason of
the teacher's religious convictions or practices. There has been real
ground for this fear ever since voluntary and publicly provided
schools first stood side by side. Section 30 provides that—

. . . no person shall be disqualified by reason of his religious opinions, or
of his attending or omitting to attend religious worship, from being a
teacher in a county school or in any voluntary school, or from being
otherwise employed for the purposes of such a school; and no teacher
in any such school shall be required to give religious instruction or receive any less emolument, or be deprived of, or disqualified for, any
promotion or other advantage by reason of the fact that he does or does
not give religious instruction or by reason of his religious opinions or of
his attending or omitting to attend religious worship.

Provided that save in so far as they require that a teacher shall not
receive any less emolument, or be deprived of, or disqualified for, any
promotion or other advantage by reason of the fact that he gives
religious instruction or by reason of his religious opinions or of his
attending religious worship, the provisions of this section shall not
apply with respect to a teacher in an aided school or with respect to a
reserved teacher in any controlled school or special agreement school.

The value of that Section depends upon the spirit in which it
is implemented. Though it is rare for an appointing body to pass
over a teacher of superior educational qualifications in favour of
one with more acceptable religious convictions, public opinion
should remain vigilant to see that, except in the cases where
qualification to give religious instruction is the prime consideration, general suitability for the post offered is always the first and
only criterion.

VII Special Educational Treatment

Sections 31 and 32 deal with the organization, management,
and maintenance of schools during the period between the coming
into operation of the Act and of the 'local education order'. Sections 33 and 34 deal with the primary and secondary education of

children handicapped by physical or mental disability who require 'special educational treatment'.

The quality and quantity of such treatment in the past varied enormously in different areas. In some it was comprehensive, kindly, and expert; in others non-existent, or slight, or indifferent in quality. The powers of the local education authority were largely permissive; they were required by law to care only for blind, deaf, mentally defective, and epileptic children. In the 1944 Act their duty was extended to cover 'any disability of mind or body' (Section 8); and more stringent directions were given in respect of both notification and treatment.

In the first place the Minister has by regulations[1] to define the various categories of pupils requiring special educational treatment, to make provision for the special methods appropriate for the education of pupils in each category, and to state the requirements to be complied with by special schools (Section 33).

It is the duty of the local education authority to ascertain what children in their area require special educational treatment (Section 34). This is a great advance on the previous law, which required the ascertainment of mental defectives and epileptics only. To carry out this duty the local education authority is granted power to require the parent of any child of two years old and upwards to submit him for examination by a medical officer. Conversely, the parent has the right to request the local education authority to examine his child. If after examination the medical officer decides that the child requires special educational treatment, the authority must so inform the parents and provide[2] the appropriate treatment. But a child is not to be 'certified' unless the issue of the certificate is necessary to secure the attendance of the child at a special school.

One item in the wording of Section 33 caused much discussion in the House of Commons during the passage of the Bill. The Section states that—

The arrangements made by a local education authority for the special educational treatment of pupils . . . shall, *so far as is practicable,*

---

[1] See *The Handicapped Pupils and Special Schools Regulations, 1959* (S.I., 1959, No. 365). See also the Ministry's pamphlet on *The Education of the Handicapped Pupil, 1945–1955.*

[2] Unless, as the Education Act, 1946, makes clear, the parent makes suitable private arrangements.

provide for the education of pupils in whose case the disability is serious in special schools; . . . but where that is impracticable, or where the disability is not serious, the arrangements may provide for the giving of such education in any school maintained or assisted by the local education authority.

One member after another of the House of Commons objected to the words I have italicized, 'so far as is practicable'. Mr (later Sir) F. Messer, the member for South Tottenham, in the course of a powerful and moving advocacy of the cause of the handicapped child, declared that—

The wording of this clause is so loose that local education authorities can easily avoid their obligation. . . . With the words 'so far as is practicable' in the clause anybody who wants to find a reason for not doing something can easily find it. (*Hansard*, 21 March 1944, Vol. 398, No. 50, cols. 690–91.)

Mr Chuter Ede, on behalf of the Government, promised consideration of an alternative wording; but no alteration was made. There has been, however, no tendency on the part of local authorities to evade their obligation; on the contrary, they have greatly extended and improved the provision for handicapped children.

VIII The Parent's Duty

Section 35 defines 'compulsory school age' as 'any age between 5 and 15 years'. But it adds:

Provided that as soon as the Minister is satisfied that it has become practicable to raise to 16 the upper limit of the compulsory school age, he shall lay before Parliament the draft of an Order in Council directing that the foregoing provisions of this section shall have effect as if for references therein to the age of 15 years there were substituted references to the age of 16 years;

and unless Parliament says 'No' within 40 days, the age will become 16.

A battle royal was waged in the House of Commons over this section, which is of course one of the key sections of the Act. A strong body of professional, public, and Parliamentary opinion pressed for a definite date for the raising of the school age of 16. The Labour Party made it one of the items of their official policy, as did also the active 'Tory Reform Group'. Mr Butler resisted every attempt, on the grounds that the uncertainties of the existing national and international situation made it impossible to fix a date with any certainty that it would be realized. He made it quite clear that on the principle of a leaving age of 16 the Government were in full agreement with the House.

I am quite sure that we are all agreed that the Bill is drafted to envisage an educational system which will enable children to remain at school until they are 16. (*Hansard*, 21 March 1944, Vol. 398, No. 59, col. 742.)

And he stressed the value of raising the age to 16. But, he continued,

we have deliberately accelerated the date at which the leaving **age** shall be introduced. . . . It is on account of the fact that raising the age will involve some improvisation that we have deliberately not put a date in the Bill for raising the age. (*Hansard*, 21 March 1944, Vol. 398, No. 50, col. 743.)

The crux of the situation, he said, lay in the reorganizing of the schools into primary and secondary. He pointed out that only 16 per cent. of the voluntary schools were reorganized into senior and junior schools, and only 62 per cent. of the council schools. In the rural areas only 20 per cent. of all schools were reorganized. To raise the school age to 15, he said, required the provision of 391,000 additional school places, to raise it to 16 a further 406,000 places. Over and above that, 150,000 school places destroyed (at that time) by enemy action had to be replaced.

When he considered the question of teachers he felt it still more wise to include no definite date for raising the school age to 16. Limitation of the size of classes to a maximum of 30 was probably one of the most important reforms to be made. To retain children between 15 and 16 in school, in classes not exceeding 30, would call for anything between 40,000 and 50,000 additional teachers, not counting replacement of wastage or the supply of teachers for county colleges.

On educational grounds the most desirable thing would be to have the age raised from 14 to 16 and the introduction at one and the same time of a system of continuing education. . . . It is absolutely essential, in my view, to see that the purview of the educational system covers the age range right up to 18. [But] it would be unwise to insist on giving raising-the-age-to-16 priority over young people's [i.e. county] colleges until we have got further with the reorganization of the schools. . . . Therefore the Government have decided . . . that authorities should plan for a period of continuing education, in the first place, from the age of 15 to 18, and thereafter, when the leaving age is raised to 16, from 16 to 18. (*Hansard*, 21 March 1944, Vol. 398, No. 50, cols. 746–7.)

No one is a more convinced advocate than I of the necessity for raising the school age to 16 at the earliest possible moment: yet I have no doubt that Mr Butler was right. To appoint 1 April 1945 as the date for the raising of the age to 15 was an exceedingly courageous gesture, but, as became apparent within a few days of the passing of the Act, an impracticable one. The date had to be postponed, and the provision in Section 105 for a delay of not more than two years was no more than sheer common sense.

The history of the years that have since elapsed has shown all too clearly how right Mr Butler was. Despite the very large number of new schools that have been built—many more than the county had ever built within the same period of time—and of teachers that have been recruited, accommodation and staffing have not kept pace with the increasing school population. Reorganization was barely complete in 1967. Compulsory part-time education and training of young people in employment has had to be delayed, and there is little likelihood that this reform will be implemented before the 1970s. To have hoped in 1944 to raise compulsory school age to 16 at any foreseeable date was, as events have conclusively demonstrated, to have hoped for the moon. Much effort and thought will be needed to raise it in 1970, the date set in 1964, and re-affirmed officially in 1967.

On the issue of part-time to 18 first or full-time to 16 I personally am convinced that Mr Butler was right. Adolescent education, whether full-time or part-time, is a whole, not two distinct and different parts; and the first essential is that up to the age of 18 boys and girls shall be ensured educational care and guidance. The beneficial effects of the rapid growth of part-time education and training on a voluntary basis since the war (to which further reference will be made later) offer, I think, incontestable evidence for this. But mine is a minority view. The Central

Advisory Council have twice advocated, in the Crowther and the Newsom Reports, that raising the school age to 16 should come first.

To the next section in the Act (Section 36) I attach the very highest importance.

It shall be the duty of the parent of every child of compulsory school age to cause him to receive efficient full-time education suitable to his age, ability, and aptitude, either by regular attendance at school or otherwise.

This section imposes a far more weighty obligation on the parent than before. Previously, all he had to do was to cause his child, between the ages of 5 and 14, 'to receive efficient elementary instruction in reading, writing, and arithmetic'. That was easy. Any elementary school would do the job. There was no obligation on the parent to know, or care, anything about the child's capacity or inclinations. But if the present obligation is taken seriously (and there is much evidence that it is), the parent must both know and care, or he will not be doing his legal duty.

The responsibility is, under the Act, a joint one. If a child is at a publicly maintained school, it is the duty of the public authorities to see that he gets an education which is both efficient and appropriate (Section 8); if he is at a private school, the Minister will guarantee that the school's premises are adequate and suitable, that the instruction is efficient and suitable, and that the proprietor and teachers are proper persons to be engaged in the education of children (Section 71). If the parent decides to educate his child himself or to put him in the charge of a private tutor, he bears the entire responsibility: but such cases are extremely rare.

Section 36 requires every parent to have a lively interest in both the duration and the quality of the education his child receives. This means that the parents of children today should have a keen interest in the introduction of compulsory part-time education and the raising of the age of compulsory full-time education to 16; and parents constitute a very influential body of public opinion which can do much to expedite and render effective such reforms.

There are many ways in which parents can exert their influence: by forming Parents' Associations, by serving on boards of managers or governors, on divisional executives and local education committees—or at least by seeing that persons who will faithfully and conscientiously represent the parents are elected to these bodies. But, above all, parents can seek to learn more about their children. That is the first essential. Far too many parents know far too little.

Section 37 deals with parents who neglect their duty. If a local education authority have reason to believe that a parent is failing to cause his child to be educated efficiently and appropriately, they will first ask him to satisfy them, within a given time (not less than a fortnight), on the point. If he does not do so, they will serve upon him a 'school attendance order' requiring him to send his child to a named school. The sovereign right of the parent is preserved in that he must be given an opportunity to choose the school himself. Failure to comply with a school attendance order renders the parent liable to prosecution.

Failure to cause a child of compulsory school age who is a registered pupil at a school to attend regularly is also a legal offence (Section 39), unless absence is due to sickness or other unavoidable cause; or to a prescribed religious observance; or if the child lives more than three miles away from the school and no suitable transport or boarding accommodation is provided by the local education authority.

In the case of children under 8 the distance is two miles. This thoughtful modification was made in the House of Lords at the insistence of Lord Gorell, who said he would press the matter to a division unless the point were conceded. For children under six, 200 attendances in a year (the equivalent of 100 days) is held to constitute 'regular attendance', and parents who by reason of their occupation have constantly to travel from place to place have only to prove that a child has attended as regularly as possible. It is such parents who, unless a child is clearly unsuited for boarding-school life, should take advantage of any boarding facilities provided by local education authorities under Section 8 of the Act. In a child's education continuity and the feeling of security which a familiar environment can give are of prime importance.

Section 40 sets out the penalties for failure to cause a child to receive efficient and appropriate education or to attend regularly at school. They are a fine not exceeding £1 for the first offence, not exceeding £5 for a second and not exceeding £10 for a third or subsequent offence. After the second offence the offender becomes liable also to imprisonment for a period of up to one month. In all cases of prosecution, whether or not the parent is convicted, the court may direct that the child be brought before a juvenile court with a view to a 'care and protection' order.

IX *Further Education*

Sections 41–47 deal with further education. This is divided in Section 41 into two categories. It is laid down here that it shall be the duty of the local education authority to secure the provision of adequate facilities for—

a   full-time and part-time education for persons over compulsory school age;

b   leisure-time occupation, in such organized cultural training and recreative activities as are suited to their requirements, for any persons over compulsory school age who are able and willing to profit by the facilities provided for that purpose.

The possibilities inherent in the above, and particularly in (*b*), are almost limitless. The Act requires (Section 42) that every authority shall prepare and submit to the Minister a scheme of further education (comparable with the Development Plan for Primary and Secondary Education), and lays down that—

A local education authority shall, when preparing any scheme of further education, have regard to any facilities for further education provided for their area by universities, educational associations, and other bodies, and shall consult any such bodies as aforesaid, and the local education authorities for adjacent areas; and the scheme, as approved by the Minister, may include such provisions as to the co-operation of any such bodies or authorities as may have been agreed between them and the authority by whom the scheme was submitted (Section 42).

This sub-section recognizes the leading part which voluntary bodies have always played in the provision of adult education, and in effect invites them to co-operate on a basis of equal partnership with the statutory authorities. It also, by its requirement of consultation between adjacent authorities, makes possible the framing of regional schemes for technical and general adult education.

X   Part-time Continued Education

The Education Act of 1918 made provision for a system of part-time education for all young persons up to the age of 18 who were not in full-time education. For the equivalent of one day a week they were to be released from their employment to attend day-time classes.

For a variety of reasons, including the hostility of both parents and employers of labour, the scheme was a failure. In few areas was it ever started, and in one only—Rugby—did it continue to operate on a statutory basis.

The 1944 Act reintroduced the proposals of the 1918 Act, with modifications designed to prevent a second failure. Section 43 lays down that—

On and after such date as His Majesty may by Order in Council determine, not later than three years after the date of the commencement of this Part of this Act,[1] it shall be the duty of every local education authority to establish and maintain county colleges, that is to say, centres approved by the Minister for providing for young persons who are not in full-time attendance at any school or other educational institution such further education, including physical, practical, and vocational training, as will enable them to develop their various aptitudes and capacities and will prepare them for the responsibilities of citizenship.

Each local authority must survey the needs of its area and submit plans for approval by the Minister, including, if necessary, provision for boarding accommodation. The Minister will then issue an order, which will be mandatory upon the authority.

It will be the duty of the local authority (Section 44) to serve upon every young person in the area who is not exempt from compulsory attendance for further education a 'college attendance order' directing him or her to attend at a specified college. The following are exempt (Section 44):

a   Anyone in full-time attendance at a school or other educational institution.

b   Anyone who is shown to the satisfaction of the local education

[1] As with the raising of the school age, a delay of up to two years is allowed for (Section 108). But up to 1 October 1967 no Order had been made.

authority to be receiving suitable and efficient instruction, full-time or part-time, equivalent to 330 hours in 12 months.

c   Anyone who does not cease to be exempt under (a) or (b) until the age of 17 years 8 months.

d   Anyone undergoing an approved course of training for the mercantile marine or the sea-fishing industry, or having completed such course is engaged in either of these occupations.

e   Any person employed by or under the Crown in any service or capacity with respect to which the Minister certifies that, because of the arrangement made for the education of young persons therein, it would be unnecessary.

f   Any person certified as a mental defective or lunatic.

g   Any person who was 15 before the coming into operation of this section, unless required by previous legislation to attend a continuation school.

The required attendance is (Section 44) one whole day or two half-days in each of 44 weeks each year, or, where the authority are satisfied that continuous attendance would be more suitable, one continuous period of 8 weeks or two continuous periods of 4 weeks each in each year. Exceptional arrangements are to be made to meet exceptional circumstances, provided that the total attendance in a year is not less than 330 hours. Unless continuous attendance is required, no person shall be asked to attend on Sunday, or a day 'exclusively set apart for religious observance by the religious body to which he belongs', or on any holiday or half-holiday to which by agreement or the custom of his employment he is entitled, or between 6 p.m. and 8.30 a.m. (In the case of night workers or persons employed at abnormal times this last provision may be modified.)

A young person who fails to comply with any of the requirements of a college attendance order, and cannot show good reason for it, is liable to prosecution and to the same penalties as parents who fail to cause their children to attend school regularly (Section 46).

Every young person not exempt from compulsory attendance for further education must keep his local education authority informed of his address. Employers must notify the authority when a young person enters or leaves their employment, and are to receive a copy of the college attendance order (Section 45).

There are two or three points in connection with this scheme of compulsory part-time education to which I would like to draw particular attention. First, the responsibility for attendance is laid upon the young person, not upon his parents. He is treated in this respect as an adult. Second, for the first time in our educational history, education for citizenship is specifically mentioned in an Act of Parliament. Third, also for the first time, the provision of residential colleges is made possible.

As to the scheme as a whole, it is perhaps sufficient to say that it is the considered opinion of many educationists and industrialists that had such a scheme been in operation since 1918, a great deal of what is popularly known as 'the youth problem' would have ceased to exist. If this be so, it is greatly to be regretted that it has not yet been brought into operation. The chances of success are far better in 1968 than in 1918. There is far less opposition from industry; in fact, so convinced are many industrialists of the need for part-time (and full-time) education and training for young employees that over 100 industries and large numbers of firms have promoted schemes of their own.[1] There would not be the previous niggardly provision of premises, staff, and equipment by education authorities. Nor would there be the opposition from parents that there was in 1918 and after. This was largely based on economic grounds; parents resented the deductions from their children's wages made or threatened by employers. As it is now agreed that no deductions shall be made, this objection is removed. Finally, I hope there would not be opposition from the students themselves. This would depend on how they were treated. If they found themselves regarded as children back at school, of course they would be dissatisfied. If, as in most of the voluntary schemes, they were regarded and treated as young men and women, they could be expected to be happy and industrious.[2]

It is possible that the training schemes projected under the Industrial Training Act, 1964, will take the place of the continued education projected by the Education Act, 1944. Time alone will show. But any system of universal part-time education has boundless possibilities. No doubt the time allocated in the 1944 Act

[1] This was before, and is independent of, the arrangements being made under the Industrial Training Act, 1964.

[2] For an enlightened and sympathetic discussion of the problems involved, see *Youth's Opportunity: Further Education in Country Colleges* (Ministry of Education Pamphlet No. 3. H.M. Stationery Office).

would have to be expanded. One day a week is not really sufficient. This was frankly admitted in *Educational Reconstruction*, but, as Mr Chuter Ede said later, when Section 44 was being debated in the House of Commons:

> We have to realize that we are legislating in this matter in the face of a great tragedy—the failure of the sections of the Act of 1918 that were framed for a similar purpose. Therefore, I ask members not to overweight this at the moment . . . every time we add an extra day to this first day, we require an additional number of teachers . . . (*Hansard*, 23 March 1944, Vol. 398, No. 52, col. 1116.)

Was such caution justified? At the time, undoubtedly it was. Ultimately, the answer lies with the public. If we want more continued education for our adolescent sons and daughters and young employees, we must not only say so, but show that we are prepared to meet the extra cost, build the additional buildings, and throw up from among ourselves the necessary staff. The rapid increase of part-time education and training on a voluntary basis since the war has shown that a growing body of employers realize that this is not an irksome burden but an investment of the highest value. Whereas in 1939 some 41,500 young employees only were released for it during working hours, by 1966 the number had risen to over 600,000.

XI   School Health Service

In 1907 an Act of Parliament was passed requiring that every child in attendance at a publicly maintained school should be medically examined at intervals during his school career. The operation of that Act effected nothing less than a revolution in the health and physique of the nation. This notwithstanding certain very hampering limitations upon the School Medical Service, as it was then called. It was able to provide certain kinds of treatment only. The duty of providing treatment was in respect of elementary school children only, and the cost of treatment had to be recovered from parents whenever possible. The 1944 Act swept away all these restrictions, and made it the duty of the local education authority—

to provide for the medical inspection, at appropriate intervals, of pupils in attendance at any school or county college maintained by them (Section 48);

and—

to make such arrangements for securing the provision of free medical treatment for pupils in attendance at any school or county college maintained by them as are necessary for securing that comprehensive facilities for free medical treatment are available to them either under this Act or otherwise (Section 48):

and—

to make arrangements for encouraging and assisting pupils to take advantage of such facilities (Section 48).

The right of the parent to refuse to make use of these facilities is safeguarded. It is a right which is rarely exercised.

By Section 78 private schools may make arrangements with the local education authority to be covered by the School Health Service. There is thus made available to every boy and girl in the country between the ages of 2 and 18 free medical inspection and medical treatment—a great advance on the previous position.

It should be noted that the School Health Service is under the ultimate control of the Minister of Health, though it is administered by the Minister of Education and the local education authorities. Section 79 of the Act requires that—

Every local education authority shall furnish to the Minister of Health such particulars as he may from time to time require of the arrangements made by the authority in the exercise of their functions relating to medical inspection and medical treatment; and that Minister may give to any such authority such directions as to the discharge by the authority of those functions as appear to him to be expedient.

Since 1948 the School Health Service has been closely linked with the National Health Service set up in that year. Local education authorities, for example, discharge their obligation to secure free hospital treatment for school children through the facilities provided by that service. The establishment of the National Health Service did not affect the medical inspection of pupils or the ascertainment of handicapped children.

XII Meals and Milk

Since 1906 local education authorities have had power to provide meals at school for children. Before the 1939–45 war this power was little exercised, save in the case of under-nourished children of necessitous parents. Rarely were more than 3 per cent. of children being provided with meals; and often the 'meal' provided was meagre, while the manner of its provision smacked of the Poor Law and public assistance. But during the war school meals became an integral part of the educational service and of the war economy. Thanks to the enlightened policy of the then Minister of Food, Lord Woolton, and the wholehearted co-operation of the President of the Board of Education, Mr R. A. Butler, a great expansion of the service began. This was continued after the war; by 1966 only 220 maintained schools had no facilities for meals. Over two-thirds of all the children in maintained schools were receiving daily a well-balanced and well-cooked midday meal at school, and over four-fifths a daily bottle of milk. About 7 per cent. of the children taking meals were getting them free.

In the Act the provision of both milk and meals is made a duty of the local education authority. Section 49 lays it down that—

Regulations[1] made by the Minister shall impose upon local education authorities the duty of providing milk, meals, and other refreshment for pupils in attendance at schools and colleges maintained by them.

Members of the House of Commons urged that the meals and milk services, like the medical service, should be free. Mr Butler's reply was that the Government would in due course announce their policy of social security, in which family allowances[2] would figure, and that then it would be necessary for the Minister of Education to fit his department's policy in respect of milk and meals into the general Government scheme.

Section 50 gives the authorities the power to provide, if necessary, boarding accommodation other than in school or college

---

[1] See *The Milk and Meals Grant Regulations, 1959.* (S.I., 1959, No. 410).

[2] The Family Allowances Act, 1945, came into operation in August 1946, when school milk was made free. See *Provision of Free Milk Regulations, 1946* (S.R. and O., 1946, No. 1293). Meals have on the contrary persistently increased in price.

for children or young persons. Section 51 gives them the power to provide a child with clothing if he 'is unable by reason of the inadequacy of his clothing to take full advantage of the education provided at the school'. This was a new power in England, though in Scotland it had obtained since 1918.

Section 53 is a most important and valuable one. It lays down that—

it shall be the duty of every local education authority to secure that the facilities for primary, secondary, and further education provided for their area include adequate facilities for recreation and social and physical training,

and—

for that purpose a local education authority, with the approval of the Minister, may establish, maintain, and manage, or assist the establishment, maintenance, and management, of camps, holiday classes, playing-fields, play-centres, and other places (including playgrounds, gymnasiums, and swimming-baths not appropriated to any school or college) at which facilities for such recreation and for such training . . . are available . . . , and may organize games, expeditions, and other activities . . . and may defray or contribute towards the expenses thereof.

When the Bill was first presented to Parliament, it was not a *duty* but merely a *power* of the local authority to secure that such facilities should be available. Those likely to benefit by them (and who is not?) have to thank Admiral Sir William James, then M.P. for North Portsmouth, for having the power converted into a duty. They should also remember that, on the authority of Mr Chuter Ede, 'The Government desire to see this clause fully implemented by the local education authorities.' (*Hansard*, 23 March 1944, Vol. 398, No. 52, col. 1166.) Sub-section (2), added in the House of Lords, requires local authorities, in arranging for such facilities, to have regard to the desirability of co-operation with voluntary bodies whose objects include the provision of similar facilities. Sub-section (3) allows the Minister to make regulations[1] empowering local education authorities to provide for pupils at a maintained school or county college 'articles of clothing suitable for the physical training provided'.

[1] See *Physical Training (Clothing) Regulations, 1945.* (S.R. and O., 1945, No. 371).

Section 54—an immensely long one—deals with evils happily diminishing in extent: foulness of person or clothing and infestation with vermin. And how difficult it was to draft! It was withdrawn by the Government during the Committee stage, and considerably modified before it was reintroduced. I trust that in its present form it will offend the susceptibilities of no one—though this is probably too much to hope. A main concern is to cause no undue embarrassment to parents of unfortunate children who, themselves clean, become infested with vermin by children of less clean parents.

Section 55 empowers the local education authority to provide free transport where necessary for pupils at schools or county colleges and to pay reasonable travelling expenses where no transport arrangements are made. Section 56 empowers the authority to make arrangements if necessary for a child or young person to be educated otherwise than at school. Section 57 deals with children 'incapable of receiving education at school'. It is the duty of the local education authority to require the parents of any child of 2 and upwards who appears to be 'suffering from a disability of mind of such a nature or to such an extent as to make him incapable of receiving education at school' to submit the child for medical inspection by a medical officer of the authority; and if the inspection shows the child to be so incapable to report the fact to the authority for the purposes of the Mental Deficiency Act, 1913. The interests of the child's parents are safeguarded, and so also are those of other children, for it is laid down in sub-section (4) that a child shall be considered 'incapable of receiving education at school', if his disability is such 'as to make it inexpedient that he should be educated in association with other children either in his own interests or theirs'.

XIII Employment of Children and Young Persons

Sections 58–60 make the necessary adaptations in the law relating to the employment of children and young persons which are required by the raising of the compulsory school age and the institution of compulsory part-time education.

Some misunderstanding of the purpose of these sections occurred when they were debated in the House of Commons, with the result that well-meaning but pointless attempts were made to prohibit the employment of children of compulsory school age. I am entirely in sympathy with the aim, for I am convinced that for a child of compulsory school age, even if this be 16, full-time education is a sufficiently exacting and laborious day's work. But as the Chairman of the Committee reminded the Commons, 'This is an Education Bill and not a Bill relating to the employment of children and young persons.' Juvenile employment is dealt with by the Children and Young Persons Acts, and the Home Secretary is responsible for the administration of these Acts, as he is also for the administration of the Shops Acts, and the Young Persons (Employment) Acts, all of which contain provisions affecting the employment of children and young persons. Changes in the law relating to such employment cannot be made in an Education Act, save in so far as any new requirements in respect of age and hours of compulsory attendance at an educational institution necessitate modification of the law relating to juvenile employment.

XIV Fees in Secondary Schools

Section 61 contains an item which was (and still is) a matter of controversy. Sub-section (1) lays down that—

No fees shall be charged in respect of admission to any school maintained by a local education authority, or to any county college, or in respect of the education provided in any such school or college.

It will be noted that the prohibition extends only to schools maintained by a local education authority. That is the point at issue. Under the Act direct grant schools (i.e. schools which receive financial aid direct from the Department of Education and Science) retain the power to charge fees.

In the debate one body of opinion demanded the abolition of fees in all secondary schools in receipt of public funds. A smaller, but influential, body of opinion passionately defended their retention. Amendments were moved in support of both these views, but the one which provoked the crucial debate was the one moved by Mr (later Lord) Silkin, M.P. for Peckham, who proposed that after the word 'any' the words 'primary or secondary' be added. (*Hansard*, 28 March 1944, Vol. 398, No. 54, col. 1272 *et seq.*)

The issue is a social, not an educational one, and an unhappy product of our tangled educational history. This is not the place to argue it, for the purpose of this book is primarily to outline the provisions of the Education Act, with comment restricted to indicating some of its possibilities and problems. It must suffice here briefly to illustrate the opposing points of view. Mr W. G. Cove, an M.P. sponsored by the National Union of Teachers, said:

It is no good trying to burke the issue. If we have some of these schools still paying fees, then it is quite clear they will be regarded with higher esteem than other schools, and that they will be regarded as having a higher status. (*Hansard*, 28 March 1944, Vol. 398, No. 54, col. 1287.)

In reply, Mr Butler said:

Education cannot by itself create the social structure of a country. . . . I have to take the world as I find it. . . . One of the fundamental principles on which this Bill has been built is that there shall be a variety of schools. One of the varieties which I think is quite legitimate is that there shall be schools in which it is possible for parents to contribute towards the education of their children. (*Ibid.*, cols. 1302–3.)

Readers who wish to study the question in detail might well start with the two reports of the Fleming Committee. In the main report, *Public Schools and the General Educational System*,[1] they will find an historical chapter showing how fees came to be charged in secondary schools and proposals for the abolition or grading of fees in direct grant schools. In the interim report, *Fees in Secondary Schools*,[2] they will find set out the arguments for and against the abolition of tuition fees in grant-aided secondary schools.

The rest of section 61 deals with charges for boarding accommodation at maintained primary and secondary schools and county colleges. The gist of it is that parents will be asked to pay board and lodging charges 'in accordance with scales approved by the Minister', and that such charges will be remitted in case of financial hardship.

Section 62 has already been referred to.[3] Section 63 exempts educational establishments from building byelaws and Section 64 voluntary schools from payment of rates. Section 65 secures to the managers or governors of a voluntary school the income from any

[1] H.M. Stationery Office, 1944.   [2] H.M. Stationery Office, 1943.
[3] See page 25.

endowment; they are not required to pay this over to the local education authority. Section 66 empowers local education authorities to assist financially governors of aided secondary schools in respect of liabilities incurred by them before Part II of this Act came into operation.

Section 67 provides that (unless expressly provided otherwise in the Act) any dispute between a local education authority and the managers or governors of a school, or between two or more local education authorities, in respect of powers or duties under the Act, may be determined by the Minister.

Section 68, which was added to the Bill at a very late stage, empowers the Minister to intervene if he is satisfied that any local education authority or the managers or governors of any county or voluntary school are acting or proposing to act unreasonably. When the section was introduced, the opinion was expressed[1] 'that this discretionary power of the Minister ought to be checked . . . either in the Courts (of Law) or by Parliament', and later an amendment was moved to the effect that any direction made by the Minister under this section should, like the Regulations he makes, be laid before Parliament for 40 days, during which time either House might annul it.

The amendment was rejected by the Government, on whose behalf the Earl of Selborne pointed out that under the Act the Minister of Education was charged with very great responsibilities, and that in effect this section constituted him a Court of Appeal.

. . . The Minister is only to come in on the complaint of any person or otherwise (the last two words refer to the exceptional cases where no complaint has been made but where he feels he is bound to act in the public interest). . . . The real purpose of the clause is to provide some court of appeal in cases where local education authorities have acted unreasonably. (*Hansard*, 18 July 1944, Vol. 132, No. 72, col. 960.)

Lord Selborne continued:

I submit that it is absolutely necessary to have such an appeal, because there are hundreds of managers and local authorities all over the country who may have to make sometimes very difficult decisions, and there may be local factors that possibly exacerbate controversy. It would be expecting altogether too much to assume that no mistake will ever be

[1] By Lord Rankeillour. (*Hansard*, 12 July 1944, Vol. 122, No. 70, col. 864.)

made, and we should all agree that the Minister should have some power of reversing an unwise or an unfortunate decision. My noble friends say that the Minister himself ought to be subject to the check either of Parliament or of a judge. But this is a matter of administration. . . . You could not administer this or any other Act under procedure of that kind. (*Hansard*, 18 July 1944, Vol. 132, No. 72, cols. 960–61.)

I have dwelt on this point at some length because of the frequently expressed fear that the tendency today is to place too much power in the hands of Ministers of the Crown, with consesequent diminution of the powers of Parliament, the local authorities, and the public. This question of the distribution of power is supremely important for the future of our democracy, and it is only right that whenever it arises the particular instance should be scrutinized with the utmost care. The 1944 Education Act gave the Minister far greater powers than ever the President of the Board of Education had; and earlier in these pages I have indicated some of the dangers which must be faced as a result. But in the present instance I feel that the Government's argument was perfectly right. If by Act of Parliament a Minister is required to 'control and direct' a 'national policy', he must be granted the last word in the administration of that Act.

Section 69 empowers the Minister to make regulations concerning the conduct of medical inspections and examinations, including the requiring of parents to submit their children, and part-time students to submit themselves, for medical examination.

Independent Schools

WHENEVER I have to explain the provisions of the Education Act, 1944, somebody always asks, 'What is the position of the private school?' Sections 70–75, which came into operation on 30 September 1957, provide a detailed answer to that question.

Section 70 states that—

The Minister shall appoint one of his officers to be Registrar of Independent (i.e. private) Schools; and it shall be the duty of the Registrar of Independent Schools to keep a register of all independent schools, which shall be open to public inspection at all reasonable times.[1]

The proprietor of any private school must (unless exempted) apply to be registered. The registration will be provisional until the school has been inspected on behalf of the Minister, who will then confirm it (provided, of course, that the report on the school is satisfactory). If the Minister is satisfied that he has sufficient information in respect of any school or class of schools to render this procedure unnecessary, the school or schools will be exempted from it and become automatically registered (Section 70).[2]

There was considerable dissatisfaction in Parliament about this last provision, which, it was alleged, smacked of favouritism. Mr Butler explained that it was simply meant to save trouble. The Ministry, he said, would have quite enough to do inspecting schools about which they knew nothing, without adding to their work by inspecting schools they already knew (by previous inspection) to be thoroughly efficient.

There are four grounds upon which a school may be refused registration or removed from the register. These are:

[1] See *The Independent Schools Registration Regulations, 1957.* (S.I. No. 929.)
[2] See *The Independent Schools (Exemption from Registration) Order, 1957.* (S.I. No. 1173.)

a   That the school premises or any parts thereof are unsuitable for a
    school.
b   That the accommodation provided at the school premises is in-
    adequate or unsuitable, having regard to the numbers, ages, and
    sex of the pupils attending the school.
c   That efficient and suitable instruction is not being provided,
    having regard to the ages and sex of the pupils.
d   That the proprietor of the school or any teacher employed therein
    is not a proper person to be the proprietor or to be a teacher in any
    school (Section 71).

A school would not be immediately struck off the register. The
procedure is that the Minister serves upon the proprietor a 'notice
of complaint', and unless the matter complained of is deemed by
the Minister to be irremediable, the proprietor is given not less
than six months to put it right (Section 71).

The proprietor may appeal by referring the complaint to an
Independent Schools Tribunal to be set up under the Act (Section
72). The Sixth Schedule provides that this tribunal shall consist of
two panels, to be appointed by the Lord Chancellor (the 'legal
panel') and the Lord President of the Council (the 'educational
panel') respectively. Members appointed to either panel must have
appropriate qualifications. Any appeal will be determined by a
tribunal of three persons from these panels, a chairman from the
legal panel, and two members from the educational panel. The
decision of the tribunal is final.

From six months after the coming into operation of this Part
of the Act, that is, since 1 April 1958, any person conducting an
unregistered school, or who, being disqualified from acting as a
teacher, accepts or endeavours to obtain employment in any
school, has been liable, for a first offence, to a fine not exceeding
£20, for a second or subsequent offence to a fine not exceeding
£50 or up to three months' imprisonment, or both (Section 73).
Any person disqualified by an order made under the Education
(Scotland) Act, 1945, is thereby disqualified also under the Educa-
cation Act, 1944 (Education Act, 1946, Second Schedule).

A disqualified person may apply to the Minister to have his
disqualification removed, and if his application is refused may
appeal to the Independent Schools Tribunal (Section 74).

Section 75 lays down that the Lord Chancellor may, with the
concurrence of the Lord President of the Council, make rules as to

the practice and procedure to be followed with respect to the constitution, appeals to, and proceedings of, the Independent Schools
Tribunals. It states that every Order made by a Tribunal must be
open to public inspection at all reasonable times.

PART FOUR

General Provisions

I *Administrative*

THIS part contains a number of administrative and financial provisions, some of little, but others of very great, importance to the general public. Among the latter is Section 76, which I give in full.

In the exercise and performance of all powers and duties conferred and imposed on them by this Act the Minister and local education authorities shall have regard to the general principle that, so far as is compatible with the provision of efficient instruction and training and the avoidance of unreasonable public expenditure, pupils are to be educated in accordance with the wishes of their parents.[1]

It had often been complained previously that the interests of parents were neglected in educational legislation. This section was intended to remove that reproach. Its efficacy has been doubted, but it has been used with effect, though too rarely.

Section 77 lays upon the Minister the duty 'to cause inspections to be made of every educational establishment at such intervals as appear to him to be appropriate' and special inspections where desirable. For this purpose inspectors may be appointed by the Crown (not, it will be noted, by the Minister, though he recommends them; inspectors of schools and other educational establishments working for the central authority have always been *His*, or *Her*, *Majesty's* Inspectors). Local authorities may appoint local inspectors for their own areas. No person other than one of H.M. Inspectors or a person authorized by the Minister or the local education authority may inspect the religious instruction in a main-

---

[1] For a statement of the principles which the Minister of Education suggested to local education authorities should be applied to make this section effective, see Circular 83.

tained school, except that the managers or governors of a voluntary school may make arrangements for the inspection on two days in the year of denominational religious instruction (Section 77).

Sections 78 and 79 have been previously referred to.[1] Section 80 requires that the 'proprietor' of a school (which in the case of a county or voluntary school means the managers or governors, in that of a private school the person or body of persons responsible for the management of the school) must keep a register of all pupils of compulsory school age.[2] The register must be open to inspection by duly authorized persons.

Section 81 is of the greatest interest to parents. It states that regulations[3] shall be made by the Minister empowering local education authorities:

a   To defray such expenses of children attending county schools, voluntary schools, or special schools, as may be necessary to enable them to take part in any school activities.

b   To pay the whole or any part of the fees and expenses payable in respect of children attending schools at which fees are payable.

c   To grant scholarships, exhibitions, bursaries, and other allowances in respect of pupils over compulsory school age, including pupils undergoing training as teachers.

d   To grant allowances in respect of any child granted a scholarship, exhibition, bursary, or other allowance by a former authority before Part II of this Act came into operation.

The purpose of this section (and of Section 100, which confers similar powers upon the Minister) is to enable pupils 'to take advantage without hardship to themselves or their parents of any educational facilities available to them'. On the whole the terms of this section have been generously interpreted, though more so by some authorities than others.

Sections 82 and 83 empower local education authorities to conduct or assist educational research, and to organize and pay for educational conferences. Section 84 empowers them to grant-aid a university or university college 'for the purpose of improving the facilities for further education available for their area'. Those words can be interpreted very widely, and again, on the whole they have provoked generous response.

[1] See page 40.
[2] See *The Pupils' Registration Regulations, 1948* (S.I. No. 2097).
[3] *Scholarships and Other Benefits Regulations, 945.* (S.R. and O., No. 666.)

GENERAL PROVISIONS 53

Sections 85–87 deal with technical points—the power of local education authorities to accept gifts, the modification of endowment schemes, and so on.

Section 88 regulates an important matter previously unregulated. It requires every local education authority to appoint a 'fit person to be the chief education officer of the authority,' and to consult the Minister (who may veto any appointment) before doing so. Previously, chief education officers, education officers, directors of education, and secretaries for education, as they were variously called, were appointed or not according to the pleasure of the local authority,[1] and there were no agreed conditions as to the qualifications required or the terms and conditions of service. None are laid down in the Act, but the fact that the appointment is now mandatory has led to considerable clarification of these matters.

Section 89, dealing with the remuneration of teachers, has been previously referred to.[2] Section 90 empowers a local education authority, subject to confirmation by the Minister, to purchase compulsorily land within or outside its area. Section 91 requires the county borough councils to keep accounts in the same fashion as is ordained for county councils. Section 92 requires every local education authority to make to the Minister such reports and returns as he may require 'for the purpose of the exercise of his functions under the Act'. Section 93 empowers the Minister, for the same purpose, to hold local inquiries. Sections 94 and 95 deal with the production of certificates of birth and legal evidence in connection with proceedings under the Act. Section 96 covers matters consequential upon the cessation of functions by authorities which by the Act ceased to exercise them. Section 97 safeguards the rights of officers of such authorities who were on war service, and Section 98 the right to due compensation of officers who suffered financially through their authority having ceased to exercise functions. These last two sections, are, of course, now of little more than historical interest, but at the time of the passing of the Act were of prime importance to the persons concerned.

Section 99 empowers the Minister to take action should a

---

[1] Almost all authorities had an education officer, but in smaller authorities he might be an officer appointed for another purpose who regarded the supervision of the educational service as subsidiary to his main function.

[2] See pages 25 and 26.

local education authority or the managers or governors of a school fail to discharge their duty. It is to be hoped that this power will rarely, if ever, have to be exercised.

II   *Financial Provisions*

Section 100 is still crucially important, though the application of paragraph (*a*) has been radically altered by the Local Government Act, 1958.[1] The Section lays down that—

The Minister shall by regulations[2] make provision:

a   For the payment by him to local education authorities of annual grants in respect of the expenditure incurred by such authorities in the exercise of any of their functions relating to education, other than their functions relating to the medical inspection and treatment of pupils.

b   For the payment by him to persons other than local education authorities of grants in respect of expenditure incurred or to be incurred for the purposes of educational services provided by them or on their behalf or under their management or for the purposes of educational research.[3]

c   For the payment by him, for the purpose of enabling pupils to take advantage without hardship to themselves or their parents of any educational facilities available to them, of the whole or any part of the fees and expenses payable in respect of children attending schools at which fees are payable, and of sums by way of scholarships, exhibitions, bursaries, and other allowances in respect of pupils over compulsory age, including pupils undergoing training as teachers.[4]

The administration of public education in England and Wales has long been based upon a partnership between the central and the local authorities; and the sharing of expenditure is an integral part of this partnership. Up to the 1944 Act, the sharing was *in the aggregate* roughly on a fifty-fifty basis; in 1938–39 (the last normal

[1] See pages 56, 67, and 80–1.
[2] See *Education (Local Education Authorities) Grant Regulations, 1945, 1946, 1948, and 1952* for the arrangements up to 1959.
[3] *Educational Services and Research Grant Regulations, 1946.* (S.R. and O., 1946, No. 424.)
[4] See page 52, footnote 3.

year), for example, the Board of Education grant for England and Wales as a whole represented 49·36 per cent. of the net recognizable expenditure of the local education authorities. But this aggregate proportion covered a very wide variation in the grants made to individual authorities, these being calculated according to the wealth or poverty of an authority.

The interim financial arrangement made between the Ministry and the local authorities after the passing of the 1944 Act was that the aggregate grant from the Ministry should be increased to 54·36 per cent., and that in addition there should be made available by the Exchequer a sum amounting to £1,500,000–£2,000,000 a year for giving additional financial assistance to the poorer authorities. The extra 5 per cent. of grant, and the additional sum, would apply to the whole of the authorities' expenditure, including existing services, the school meals and milk service excepted. On these the previous very high rates of grant were to continue.

The critics of this arrangement (and they were many) maintained that the proposed increase in the grant from the central authority was totally inadequate to enable the local authorities to carry out their obligations under the Act. This proved to be the case. In 1948 a new formula for the main grant was introduced by which the Exchequer met approximately 64 per cent. of the local education authorities' net recognized expenditure.

The new formula was as follows—

a   A grant of 120s. per unit (i.e. child) of the average number on the registers in maintained and assisted primary and secondary schools (including special schools and nursery schools and nursery classes maintained by local authorities);
PLUS (*b*) a grant of 60 per cent. on the net recognizable expenditure of the authority;
LESS (*c*) the product of a 30*d*. rate in the £ in the area.

It will be seen that this formula related the grant directly to the number of school children in the area, raised the rate of grant on the local authority's expenditure, and included a principle— that of deducting the product of a given local rate—which secured for poorer authorities a larger grant. Poorer authorities also benefited by the provision made in the Local Government Act, 1948, for equalization grants.

The Local Government Act, 1958, abolished percentage grants for specific services and substituted a general ('block') grant for all services to each county council and county borough council. How the new procedure (which was, and is, disliked by a great many educational administrators and teachers) is operated in respect of public education is described on pages 80–1.

Paragraph (*b*) in Section 100 (1) makes provision for continued assistance by the Minister to voluntary bodies. A point of interest is that for the first time the Minister is empowered to grant-aid educational research. Paragraph (*c*) illustrates another aspect of the partnership between the central and the local authorities. It will be seen that it confers on the Minister precisely the same powers, and for the same purpose, as are conferred upon the local authorities by Section 81.

The final sub-section of Section 100 provides that—

Nothing in this section shall affect any grants in aid of university education payable out of moneys provided by Parliament otherwise than in accordance with the provisions of this Act.

Universities and university colleges are outside the scope of this Act, as they have been of all Education Acts. They are not part of the statutory system of education, but autonomous bodies—despite the fact that since 1919 a large proportion of their income has come from public funds.

Section 101 deals with the payment of grants by the Minister to the local education authorities in Wales and Monmouthshire. Here also the procedure for payment has been altered by the Local Government Act, 1958.

Section 102 has previously been referred to.[1] It is the financial basis of the compromise between the Minister and the religious denominations.

Section 103 makes a valuable concession to managers or governors of voluntary schools which for one reason or another have to be transferred to another site. It provides that in such case the Minister will make a grant of up to 50 per cent.[2] in aid of the construction of the new school (or schools, if more than one is to

[1] See page 19.
[2] Raised to 75 per cent. by the Education Act, 1959, and to 80 per cent. by the Education Act, 1967.

be built to replace the discontinued one). This grant will cover also expenditure upon the acquisition of the new site. Special agreement schools will, under Section 102, be grant-aided in accordance with the special agreement in respect of each school.

Section 104 makes a similar provision[1] to Section 103 to enable the Minister to grant-aid the construction of a new school required, in whole or in part, to provide accommodation for a substantial number of displaced pupils,' that is, pupils left without a school owing to the closure of an old school. The grant will be only in respect of the accommodation required for the displaced pupils, not in respect of the entire premises.

Section 105 made a valuable concession to the religious denominations. It was included in the Bill at a late stage, and was due to the persistent representations of the denominations that the expenditure they were forced to contemplate as a result of the Act was quite beyond their means unless some measures were found to ease the burden. It must be added that the section was regarded with apprehension by the opponents of Dual Control.

In brief, the section provides that where the Minister is satisfied that the initial expenses required to alter satisfactorily the premises of an aided or special agreement school involve capital expenditure which ought properly to be met by borrowing, he may make a loan to the managers or governors at a rate of interest and on such terms and conditions as may be agreed between him and them with the consent of the Treasury. It was understood that this would mean that the managers or governors of voluntary schools would be able to secure loans on terms similar to those conceded to local authorities.

So that there may be no mistake as to what expenditure is covered, the section defines 'initial expenses,'[2] and the share of these for which the managers or governors are responsible. It also contains a sub-section of the highest importance to the Nonconformists, whose grievance it was for many years that in some thousand of parishes the only school was a Church of England school, and that therefore in the parishes they were compelled to

---

[1] Similarly raised progressively to 75 per cent. and 80 per cent.

[2] The definition is enlarged by the Education Act, 1959, to include 'any expenses in respect of which the Minister may make a grant' towards the establishment of a secondary school. See page 112.

submit their children to a form of religious instruction which they found distasteful.

The sub-section provides that if an application is made to him for an order directing that a school shall be an aided or special agreement school, and it appears to him that the area concerned will not be served by a county or a controlled school, then before considering a loan to the managers or governors—

the Minister shall consult such persons or bodies of persons as appear to be representative of any religious denomination which, in his opinion, having regard to the circumstances of the area, are likely to be concerned (Section 105),

and may further, if necessary, cause a local inquiry to be held before he decides whether or not to make a loan.

At the time of the passing of the Bill the interesting point was raised that many persons likely to be concerned might not be members of any religious denomination. Were they to be called into consultation? The wording of the section apparently rules them out; but unless the Minister is satisfied that a public inquiry is unnecessary he must institute one, and this affords any such interested persons ample opportunity to make representations.

Section 106 provides for payment between local authorities in the case of children and young persons resident in the area of one authority and being educated in the area of another.[1] Such cases are, of course, numerous. Section 107 enables Parliament to meet the expenditure of the Minister of Education and the Minister of Health under this Act.

[1] The scope of this Section was broadened by the Education Act, 1946, to cover, not only the provision of education, but also 'any benefits or services for which provision is made by or under the enactments relating to education'. The intricate business of recoupment to a local education authority of the cost of providing education for persons not belonging to their area was dealt with in the 1948 and 1953 Acts. The *Local Education Authorities Recoupment (Primary, Secondary and Further Education) Amending Regulations, 1959* (S.I. 1959, No. 448) lay down that the cost shall be shared amongst all the local education authorities by adjustment of the general grant.

Supplemental Provisions

MANY of the sections in this part are concerned with the bringing into operation of the Act and with its application or non-application to various persons and places.

Section 108 provides that the Minister may authorize or require a local authority or other body to anticipate any provisions of the Act in order to expedite the coming into operation of the Part of the Act concerned. He may, if necessary, constitute for this purpose joint education boards, joint education committees, or divisional executives. On the other hand, the section empowers the Minister to delay the raising of the school age from 14 to 15 and the establishment of county colleges for not more than two years. As has been already noted, advantage was taken of this provision.

Section 109 empowers the Minister to authorize local education authorities to provide or assist in providing temporary accommodation to voluntary schools in order to facilitate the coming into operation of Part II of the Act.

Section 110, added at a late stage, is now of historical interest only, but until the introduction of the revised grant formula and Exchequer Equalization grants was exceedingly important. It dealt with the transitional period only, a period, as may be imagined, of difficult adjustment. The gist of the clause is that if the transfer of powers from the Part III authorities to the county authorities was shown to bring about excessive variations in the rates as from district to district, the Minister could, after the circumstances had been investigated, make adjustment to prevent such variations. The permissible adjustments, and the procedure of making them, are laid down in the Seventh Schedule of the Act, to which interested readers are referred.

Section 111 provides that the Minister, the Minister of Health, or a local education authority may vary or revoke any order or directions they have made or given under the Act, though if such order or directions have involved the consent or consultation of any person or persons, there must be further consent or consultation before any variation or revocation can be made.

Much has been heard in recent years about the danger of 'government by regulations', and widespread anxiety expressed lest Ministers of the Crown should take or be granted over-large powers to make regulations. The safeguard against this danger, in education law, is stated in Section 112—

All regulations made under this Act shall be laid before Parliament as soon as may be after they are made, and if either House of Parliament, within the period of 40 days beginning with the day on which any such regulations are laid before it, resolves that the regulations be annulled, the regulations shall cease to have effect, but without prejudice to anything previously done thereunder or to the making of new regulations.

The period of 40 days is not to include any days on which Parliament is dissolved or prorogued, or any time during which both Houses are adjourned for more than four days.

Section 113, as amended by the Education Act, 1946, provides that any order, notice, or other document served upon anyone under the Act shall go to his usual or last-known address.

Section 114 is the 'interpretation' section—and not unnaturally the longest in the Act. I extract from it a few of the more important definitions not previously elucidated in these pages.

'Agreed syllabus' means[1] an agreed syllabus of religious instruction prepared in accordance with the provisions of the Fifth Schedule.

'Alterations' (as amended by the Education Act, 1946), in relation to any school premises, includes any improvements or enlargements which do not amount to the establishment of a new school.

'Child' means a person who is not over compulsory school age.[2]

[1] Except in the cases referred to in sub-section (4) of this section, which allows a previously adopted syllabus to stand.

[2] Sub-section (5) of this section provides that a person in attendance at a school or county college who attains any age during a term shall not be deemed to have attained the age until the end of the term.

'Clothing' includes footwear.

'County' means an administrative county.

'Independent school' means any school at which full-time education is provided for five or more pupils of compulsory school age (whether or not such education is also provided for pupils under or over that age), not being a school maintained by a local education authority or a school in respect of which grants are made by the Minister to the proprietor of the school.

'Parent,' in relation to any child or young person, includes a guardian and every person who has the actual custody of the child or young person.

'Premises', in relation to any school, includes any detached playing-fields, but, except where otherwise expressly stated, does not include a teacher's dwelling-house.

'Proprietor', in relation to any school, means the person or body of persons responsible for the management of the school, and for the purposes of the provisions of this Act relating to applications for the registration of independent schools includes any person or body of persons proposing to be so responsible.

'Young person' means a person over compulsory school age who has not attained the age of 18 years.[1]

The above should be taken as illustrative of the definitions in this section. An important later sub-section provides that so long as any county or voluntary school is providing both primary and secondary education it shall be officially regarded as a primary school. The Minister may relax this rule if the primary education is given in a separate department.

Section 115 provides that the Act shall not apply to any person employed by or under the Crown if the Minister is satisfied that the arrangements made for the education of children and young persons within that particular service render it unnecessary, Section 116 that the Act shall not apply to persons under the Lunacy and Mental Deficiency Acts, Section 122 that it shall not apply to Scotland or Northern Ireland.

Section 117 treats of the application of the Act to the county of London, where, for example, the term 'minor authority' has to

[1] But see page 60, footnote 2.

be understood to mean the City of London or a metropolitan
borough. Section 118 provides that the Minister shall by order
make the Act applicable to the Isles of Scilly as though these were
a separate county.

Section 119 provides that Parts I and V of the Act come into
operation on the passing of the Act, Parts II and IV on 1 April
1945, and Part III on a date after that to be appointed by an Order
in Council.

Section 120 and the Eighth Schedule provide for the necessary amendments, Section 121 and the Ninth Schedule the repeal
of previous legislation. Finally, Section 122 provides that the Act
may be cited as 'The Education Act, 1944'.

Schedules

First Schedule. Local Administration. This schedule is in three
parts, dealing respectively with the establishment of Joint Education Boards, the establishment and constitution of education
committees (including joint committees), and the delegation
of functions of local education authorities to divisional executives.

Part III of the First Schedule was considerably altered by the
Education Act, 1946; the changes will be found in the Second
Schedule of that Act.

*Second Schedule. Transfer to a local education authority of an
interest in the premises of a voluntary school.* The schedule provides
that while a local education authority and the managers or governors of any voluntary school which is maintained by the authority
may make an agreement for such transfer, this will not take effect
until it has been approved by the Minister, who has to be satisfied
that due notice has been given to all persons concerned, and to
consider any representations made.

*Third Schedule. Special agreements in respect of certain voluntary
schools.* This provides for the revival of agreements proposed, but

not carried into effect, under the Education Act, 1936. All agreements must be approved by the Minister. See also the Education Act, 1948, First Schedule.

Fourth Schedule. Meetings and Proceedings of Managers and Governors. Details of constitution and procedure.

Fifth Schedule. Procedure for preparing and bringing into operation an agreed syllabus of religious instruction. Lays down that the local education authority must convene a conference representative of—

a such religious denominations as in the opinion of the authority ought, having regard to the circumstances of the area, to be represented;

b except in the case of an area in Wales or Monmouthshire, the Church of England;

c such associations representing teachers as, in the opinion of the authority ought, having regard to the circumstances of the area, to be represented; and

d the authority.

Sixth Schedule. Constitution of Independent Schools Tribunal. See page 49.

Seventh Schedule. Adjustment of variations of rates consequent upon commencement of Part II of this Act. See page 59.

Eighth Schedule. Amendments of Enactments.

Ninth Schedule. Enactments Repealed.

Making the Act Work

Here, then, in very brief is the outline of this profoundly important Act. I have been compelled for reasons of space to omit reference to numerous points of detail. But this book does not pretend to be a comprehensive exposition and commentary. It is

ɔnly to give a quick, and I hope readable, digest. Readers
ʌsh a fuller exposition are referred to *The Education Act,
1944; being a Supplement to Owen's Education Acts Manual* (C.
Knight), and to *The New Law of Education,* by M. M. Wells and
P. S. Taylor (Butterworth). In both cases the latest edition should
be consulted.

May I end as I began, by reminding you that 'legislation can
do little more than prepare the way for reform'? Though much
has been done, the utmost resolution, skill, effort, and goodwill
will continue to be required to bring this massive Act fully into
operation, ensure its smooth administration, and above all secure
that the spirit with which its provision were conceived is kept
alight.

Checkin Receipt
Lanchester Library
University of Coventry

Title: Media & society : an introduction
ID: 38001002580094
Circulation system messages:
Item returned

Title: Studying the media :
ID: 38001005116904
Circulation system messages:
Item returned

Total items: 2
25/03/2010 17:27

Some Important Regulations made by the Minister under the Education Act, 1944

NOTE.—Amending Regulations, which are made frequently, are only included if of exceptional importance. They are normally incorporated in the new bodies of Regulations issued from time to time. These revoke previous Regulations, but some of the latter are retained here for their historical interest.

No.	Date	Title
937	10.viii.44	The Education (Date of Appointment of Minister) Order, 1944.
979	17.viii.44	The Compulsory School Age (Postponement) Order 1944.
1415	13.xii.44	Schemes of Divisional Administration (Notices) Regulations, 1944.
1470	29.xii.44	School Attendance Order Regulations, 1944.
152	7.ii.45	Central Advisory Councils for Education Regulations, 1945.
248	28.ii.45	County and Voluntary Schools (Notices) Regulations, 1945.
185	6.ii.45	Welsh Special Grant Regulations, 1945.
255	6.iii.45	The Education (Welsh Annual Payments) Order, 1945.
2037	8.ix.48	Central Welsh Board Amending and Revocation Regulations, 1948.
345	24.iii.45	Standards for School Premises, 1945.
1753	28.ix.51	——1951.
473	26.iv.54	——1954.
890	27.v.59	——1959.
371	24.iii.45	Physical Training (Clothing) Regulations, 1945.
2222	4.x.48	The Provision of Clothing Regulations, 1948.
439	17.iv.45	Registration of Pupils at Schools Regulations, 1945.
2097	14.ix.48	The Pupils' Registration Regulations, 1948.
542	3.v.45	Educational Research Grant Regulations, 1945.
424	22.iii.46	Educational Services and Research Grant Regulations, 1946.
1509	9.ix.46	The Soke of Peterborough and City of Peterborough Joint Education Board Order, 1946.
636	29.v.45	Primary and Secondary Schools (Grant Conditions) Regulations, 1945.
1743	28.ix.51	The Schools Grant Regulations, 1951.
666	17.v.45	Scholarships and Other Benefits Regulations, 1945.
1216	23.vii.46	State Scholarships and University Supplemental Awards Regulations, 1946.
1406	3.vii.47	——1947.

No.	Date	Title
1655	15.vii.48	——1948.
1471	9.vii.47	Technical State Scholarships Regulations, 1947.
1629	13.vii.48.	——1948.
1472	9.vii.47	State Scholarships (Mature Students) Regulations, 1947
1214	5.vii.51	The State Scholarships Regulations, 1951.
957	22.vii.54	——1954.
1288	26.vii.46	Art Awards Regulations, 1946.
1292	27.vii.46	Science Awards Regulations, 1946.
627	15.iv.50	——1950.
698	6.vi.45	Provision of Milk and Meals Regulations, 1945.
1293	27.vii.46	Provision of Free Milk Regulations, 1946.
699	6.vi.45	Educational Conferences Regulations, 1945.
709	13.vi.45	Education (Local Education Authorities) Grant Regulations, 1945.
1215	23.vii.46	——1946.
334	23.ii.48	——1948.
1331	16.vii.52	——1952.
318	28.ii.49	The Local Education Authorities (Recoupment) Regulations, 1949.
507	23.iii.53	——1953.
815	21.vi.54	The Local Education Authorities Recoupment (Further Education) Regulations, 1954.
1076	26.vii.45	Handicapped Pupils and School Health Service Regulations, 1945.
1156	27.vii.53	The School Health Service and Handicapped Pupils Regulations, 1953.
1302	15.x.45	Handicapped Pupils (Certificate) Regulations, 1945.
1805	8.xii.53	——1953.
352	13.iii.46	Further Education Grant Regulations, 1946.
1291	27.vii.46	Ministry of Education (Further Education and Training) Grant Regulations, 1946.
1353	2.viii.46	The Employment of Children in Entertainments Amending Rules, 1946.
1742	22.vii.48	The Youth Employment Service (Administrative Expenses) Regulations, 1948. (Made by the Minister of Labour).
	1.ii.45	Training Colleges (Capital Grants) Provisional Grant Regulations, 1945.
	29.iii.45	Teachers' Emergency and Special Training Grant Provisional Regulations, 1945.
1657	31.vii.47	Teachers' Emergency and Special Training Regulations, 1947.
630	29.iv.46	Training of Teachers Grant Regulations, 1946.
1704	22.vii.48	——1948.
1203	21.vii.50	——1950.
1907	16.xii.55	——1955.
1289	26.vii.46	Training of Teachers Supplementary Grant Regulations, 1946.

No.	Date	Title
1317	23.x.45	Remuneration of Teachers Order, 1945.
1898	1.x.46	——1946.
551	8.iii.48	——1948.
300	15.iii.54	The Remuneration of Teachers (Primary and Secondary Schools) Order, 1954.
1440	1.x.56	——1956.
1441	1.x.56	The Remuneration of Teachers (Further Education) Order, 1956.
889	28.iv.48	National Insurance (Modification of Teachers' Pensions) Regulations, 1948.
1482	1.x.56	Amending Regulations, 1956.
468	17.iii.49	Teachers' Superannuation (National Service) Rules, 1949.
216	10.ii.50	The Superannuation (Civil Servants and Teachers) Rules, 1950.
1512	1.x.56	The Teachers' Superannuation (Allocation of Pension) Rules, 1956.
1514	1.x.56	The Teachers' Superannuation (Service in Schools Abroad) Rules, 1956.
1481	1.x.56	The Teachers' Superannuation (Accepted Schools) Rules, 1956.
1297	1.viii.57	The Teachers' Superannuation (Previous Employment) Rules, 1957.
604	29.iii.49	The Teachers' Registration Council Revoking Order, 1949.
Rules	16.v.49	Recognition of Schools, etc., as efficient. Revised May 1949.
472	20.iii.51	The Local Authorities and Local Education Authorities (Allocation of Functions) Regulations, 1951. (Made jointly by Home Office and Education Department under the Children Act, 1948).
929	30.ix.57	The Independent Schools Registration Regulations, 1957.
1173	30.ix.57	The Independent Schools (Exemption from Registration) Order, 1957.

LOCAL GOVERNMENT ACT, 1958

In consequence of this Act, which replaced percentage grants to local education authorities by general grants to county and county borough councils, the following important bodies of Regulations were issued by the Minister of Education. All came into operation on 1 April 1959.

No.	Title
447	The General Grants (Pooling Arrangements) Regulations, 1959.
448	The Local Education Authorities Recoupment (Primary, Secondary and Further Education) Amending Regulations, 1959.
364	The Schools Regulations, 1959.
393	The Further Education (Local Education Authorities) Regulations, 1959.
394	The Further Education (Grant) Regulations, 1959.

No.	Title
395	The Training of Teachers (Local Education Authorities) Regulations, 1959.
396	The Training of Teachers (Grant) Regulations, 1959.
363	The School Health Service Regulations, 1959.
410	The Milk and Meals Grant Regulations, 1959.
365	The Handicapped Pupils and Special Schools Regulations, 1959.
366	The Special Schools and Establishments (Grant) Regulations, 1959.
362	The Handicapped Pupils (Boarding) Regulations, 1959.
336	The Medical Examinations (Sub-normal Children) Regulations, 1959.

LATER REGULATIONS

No.	Date[1]	Title
1832	6.xi.59	The Direct Grant Schools Regulations, 1959.
708	1.xi.60	The Training of Teachers (Local Education Authorities) Amending Regulations, 1960.
1689	1.ix.62	The University and Other Awards Regulations, 1962.
1234	20.vii.63	The Remuneration of Teachers (Primary and Secondary Schools) Order, 1963.
1233	20.vii.63	The Remuneration of Teachers (Further Education) Order, 1963.
1468	3.ix.63	The Schools (Amending) Regulations, 1963.
3	9.i.65	The Schools Amending Regulations, 1965.
603	1.iv.65	Transfer of Functions (Cultural Institutions) Order, 1965.
1404	1.ix.65	The University and Other Awards Regulations, 1965.
1577	1.i.67	The Schools Amending Regulations, 1966.
792	6.vi.67	The Training of Teachers Regulations, 1967.
1305	4.ix.67	Remuneration of Teachers (Primary and Secondary Schools) Order, 1967.

Copies may be bought direct from H.M.S.O. or through a bookseller.

[1] Of coming into operation.

Extracts from Regulations

In the following pages is given a brief résumé of important points in some of the main bodies of Regulations.

Central Advisory Councils

The term of office of the Chairman of each Council is three years, that of any other member three years. The Minister may prolong the term, and a Chairman or any other member may be re-appointed.

A member absent from three consecutive meetings except for a reason approved by the Minister thereby vacates his office.

Each Council may appoint such committees as they think fit and include with the Minister's consent persons not members of the Council.

Welsh Special Grant

These Regulations repealed the Welsh Intermediate Education Act Regulations, 1930 (a), but provided that the total amount of the Welsh special grants for any year in respect of the schools situated within the area of any county or county borough should be equal to the maximum amount which was payable in respect of those schools under Section 9 of the Welsh Intermediate Education Act, 1889.

Standards for School Premises

The 1945 Building Regulations prescribed general standards for all primary and secondary schools and particular standards for different types of schools. They were applicable to both existing and new schools, and covered county and voluntary schools, nursery schools and classes, special schools, and boarding accommodation. The prescribed standards were *minimum* standards.

The Regulations were framed on the basis of an ultimate school-leaving age of 16, but while plans were to be drawn on this basis, it was not contemplated that accommodation required solely or mainly for raising the age from 15 to 16 would be provided.

Fresh bodies of Regulations were issued in 1951, 1954 and 1959. These did not substantially alter the picture; they reduced some requirements and stiffened others, but in general made the Regulations simpler and more flexible, so as to encourage experiment in design and construction. The following notes are based on the 1959 Regulations.

Sites and Playgrounds

Primary school sites range from $\frac{1}{2}$ acre for a school of not more than 25 pupils to 2 acres for 480; beyond that number, individual approval. Secondary school sites are from $1\frac{1}{2}$ acres for up to 150 pupils to 3 acres for 450; beyond that, $\frac{1}{4}$ acre per 50 pupils. Every primary school must have a paved area, ranging from 3,200 square feet (infant school up to 100 pupils) to 24,200 square feet (junior school of 361–480), and (except infant schools) playing field accommodation ranging from $\frac{1}{2}$ acre to 3 acres. Secondary school paved and playing field areas are much larger; for example, 10 acres of playing field for a mixed school of 301–600, with an additional $1\frac{1}{4}$ acres for every 120 pupils of 16 and upwards. A nursery school site must not be less than $\frac{1}{4}$ acre for up to 40 children, and must include garden playing space of not less than 100 square feet per child.

Size of Classrooms

The Regulations specify minimum areas of teaching accommodation for so many pupils (e.g., 50 square feet each for the first 40 pupils and 17 square feet a pupil thereafter in a primary school of 120 or more pupils, and 44, 47, and 50 square feet for each pupil of 11–13, 14–15, and 16 and over in a secondary school of 451–600 pupils.

Every primary school designed for 100 pupils or more must have a hall. Accommodation for secondary schools must include a hall, gymnasium, library, and accommodation for practical instruction. In a one- or two-form entry school hall and gymnasium may be combined.

In every primary and secondary school suitable accommodation must be immediately available at any time during school hours for the inspection and treatment of pupils by doctors, dentists, and nurses. Dining and kitchen accommodation (or serving and washing up accommodation if the meals are cooked elsewhere) must be provided. There must be staff common rooms for teachers, and except in primary schools with not more than 120 pupils a separate room for the head teacher.

Special Schools

For special schools, sites range from $\frac{1}{2}$ acre for a school of not more than 25 pupils to $\frac{3}{4}$ acre for one of 51–80 pupils; after that, $\frac{1}{8}$ acre per 40 pupils, or more for senior pupils. For boarding schools sites are larger, each case being considered separately.

The site of every special school must include a paved area, of dimensions rather more generous than those for normal schools. Every special school for educationally sub-normal pupils of both sexes and all ages must have playing-field accommodation adjoining the site of the school (unless otherwise approved). Teaching accommodation is 5,600 sq. ft. for the first 100 pupils and 600 square feet for each subsequent 20 pupils.

The Regulations for accommodation for meals, staff rooms, medical inspection and treatment, and storage space are the same as those for schools for normal children.

Boarding Accommodation

The area of every site for boarding accommodation is a matter for individual approval.

In dormitories there must be a floor area of not less than 55 sq. ft. each for the first two beds and 45 for each after these. Beds must be not less than 3 ft. apart. Boarding accommodation must include day room space at the rate of not less than 25 sq. ft. a pupil (in some conditions this may be relaxed), and a sickroom containing one bed for every 20 boarders; if there are more than 40 boarders a separate isolation room must be provided.

In 1959 three new regulations were added, to ensure respectively that buildings were adequate to resist bad weather, that the acoustics were appropriate, and that there was a sufficiency of gas and electric power points. As before, there are detailed regulations about lighting, heating, ventilation, water supply, sanitation, drainage and sewage disposal.

Educational Research

The Minister may make grants to any recognized persons other than local education authorities in respect of expenditure incurred or to be incurred for—

a   Development of special educational methods;
b   Maintenance of special educational services of an advisory or organizing character;
c   Research.

Persons seeking recognition must satisfy the Minister as to—

a   The precise purpose for which the service or research is being, or is to be, conducted;
b   Their financial standing;
c   Generally, their fitness to receive grant.

Any premises or other thing used for research or service shall be open to inspection by Her Majesty's Inspectors, and such records must be kept and information and returns furnished as the Minister may require.

Primary and Secondary Schools

All maintained school premises must be kept in a proper state of repair, cleanliness, and hygiene, and have adequate precautions against danger from fire and other dangers to health and safety. The Secretary of State's approval is required for the giving of instruction involving the use of radio-active substances and equipment, other than television sets, producing X-rays.

Nothing whatever is said in the Regulations about the curriculum. There must be a timetable showing the times at which the school sessions begin and end, and the place of any instruction regularly given elsewhere than at the school.

A nursery school must have a superintendent teacher, every

other school or department a head teacher, and every school a staff of assistant teachers suitable and sufficient in number for providing full-time education suitable to the ages, abilities, and aptitudes of the children. Save for exceptions stated in the Regulations, all must be qualified teachers.

Public Examinations

Until 1963 pupils under the age of 16 might not be entered for public examinations unless the Head Teacher certified that it was educationally desirable for them to do so, and that they were likely to pass. S.I. 1963 No. 1468 permitted entry for pupils who had completed or were about to complete a fifth year of secondary education.

Employment of Teachers

In order to be qualified a teacher must have completed to the Minister's satisfaction an approved course of training, or possess some special qualifications approved by the Minister.

He must satisfy the Minister as to his health and physical capacity for teaching.

He must normally serve one year on probation. A person not a qualified teacher who is 18 years old and has passed an approved examination, or possesses some other qualification approved by the Minister, may be employed as a temporary assistant teacher, normally for a period not exceeding two years. In emergency, or part-time, unqualified persons may be employed as occasional teachers.

A qualified or temporary teacher must be employed under either a written agreement or a minute of the employing local education authority. He must be given a copy of the minute or agreement, which must provide that he shall not be required to perform any duties except such as are connected with the work of the school or abstain outside school hours from any occupations which do not interfere with the due performance of his duties.

Admission

A pupil shall not be refused admission to or excluded from a school on other than reasonable grounds.

Save in exceptional circumstances, a pupil shall not be admitted to a nursery school under the age of 2 years or to a nursery class under the age of 3 years, or be retained over the age of 5 years in either. A nursery school may, however, be approved for pupils up to 7 years.

Size of Classes

The maximum number of pupils on the register of any class shall be:

For a nursery class, 30.
For a class in a primary school, 40 (but if the class consists mainly of senior pupils, 30).
For any class in a secondary school of any type, 30.

If, owing to the shortage of teachers or other unavoidable circumstances, it is not possible to keep within these limits, the numbers are to be such as is reasonable in the circumstances.

Leave of absence may not be granted to enable a pupil to be employed during school hours except under arrangements approved by the Minister permitting such employment temporarily because he considers that the general welfare of the community justifies them, or in accordance with a licence granted under section 22 of the Children and Young Persons Act, 1933. Leave of absence for not more than two weeks during a school year may be granted if a parent desires the pupil to accompany him on his annual holiday.

Before 1967 the school year had to be divided into three or four terms, but S.I. 1966 No. 1577 removed the obligation to have any specified number of terms. In a year a school must meet for at least 400 sessions (a day being divided into a morning and an afternoon session). Occasional holidays during term-time may be granted up to the extent of 20 sessions.

Direct-grant Grammar Schools

The criterion for admission of all pupils in any direct-grant grammar school shall be the capacity of the pupil to profit by education in the school. To secure that no pupil shall be precluded from entrance because of the inability of his parent to pay fees—

a the governors shall make adequate arrangements for ensuring that no pupil who is incapable of profiting by the education in the school shall be admitted thereto or retained therein; that the minimum educational standard for admission or retention shall be the same for all pupils of similar age; that preference in admission shall be given to candidates considered likely to profit most by the education in the school.

Provided that such preference shall not affect—

i the award of a minimum percentage of free places as required by these Regulations;
ii any arrangements made between the governors and authorities for the admission of pupils;
iii any preference in admission prescribed by any scheme relating to the school; or
iv in the case of a school attached to an institution, any requirement that pupils in the school shall be members of the institution.
b The governors shall each year offer to pupils who have at any time previously attended a grant-aided primary school for not less than two years free places to the extent of not less than 25 per cent. of the admissions to the upper school during the previous year. Such free places may be offered directly by the governors or through a local education authority;
c If in any year the number of free places which the governors desire to offer through the agency of the authority for any area served by the school is insufficient for the needs of that authority, the authority may, not later than six months before the beginning of the next educational year, require the governors to put at their disposal 'reserved places'. The aggregate number of free and re-served places filled in any year shall not, except with the consent of the governors, exceed 50 per cent. of the admissions to the upper school during the previous year;
d The remaining places in the upper school, called 'residuary places', shall be filled by the governors in accordance with paragraph (a) of this Regulation. The approved fees will be payable in respect of pupils holding residuary places, but if the parent of any such pupil, not a boarder, applies for total or partial remission of fees, the governors shall make such remission as the parent is entitled to under the approved income scale;

The fees for pupils holding free or reserved places through an authority shall be paid by the authority;

In addition to the capitation grant payable under these Regulations the Minister will pay for each educational year a grant equal to the difference between the amount of the approved fees which could have been charged to the holder of a residuary place and the amount actually charged.

Subject to the provisions of these Regulations, a capitation grant will be payable by the Minister for each educational year in respect of each pupil in the upper school between the ages of 10 and 19 at the beginning of the educational year. (The amount of grant is revised from time to time.)

Governing Bodies

The scheme regulating a direct-grant grammar school must provide for—

> either (a) the appointment of not less than one-third of the governors by the authority in whose area the school is situated, or the authorities served by the school;
>
> or (b) the appointment of a majority of representative governors by the persons for the time being responsible for carrying on the school.

Financial Aid for School Pupils

To enable pupils to take advantage without hardship to themselves or their parents of any educational facilities available to them every local education authority may—

a   Defray such expenses of children attending county schools, voluntary schools, or special schools as may be necessary to enable them to take part in any school activities.

b   Pay the approved fees of children attending direct-grant schools, whether within or outside the area of the authority, at which fees are payable.

c   Defray the expenses payable in respect of children attending direct-grant schools, whether within or outside the area of the authority, at which fees are payable.

d   Pay the whole or part of the approved fees and expenses of children attending schools, whether within or outside the area of the authority, which are not in receipt of direct grant and at which fees are payable.

e   Grant scholarships, exhibitions, bursaries, or other allowances in respect of pupils over compulsory school age attending schools. The expenses under (*a*) do not include clothing such as authorities may provide under the Education Act, 1948.

Particulars of the arrangements made by the authority must by approved by the Minister. Payments under (*b*) and (*d*) above may in certain conditions cover boarding or lodging fees. The authority must be satisfied that the pupils will pursue a suitable course for a definite period.

Awards for Higher Education

The Education Act, 1962, imposed on local education authorities an obligation to make awards to enable students to attend 'designated' courses at universities and establishments of further education. Designated courses include full-time university courses and courses of comparable standing, and the educational qualifications requisite for an award include passes at advanced level in two subjects in the G.C.E. (or comparable Scottish or Northern Ireland examinations), or a good Ordinary National Certificate or Diploma. The L.E.As. are also mainly responsible for grants to students pursuing an approved course of training as teachers.

The Minister has awarded annually since 1947 State scholarships for mature students, and from 1957 State scholarships for post-graduate study, called State studentships.

To be eligible for a Mature Student's scholarship a candidate must be over 25, and—

a   be ordinarily resident in England or Wales at the date of the award;

b   satisfy the Minister that he is likely to benefit by a full-time honours degree course;

c   have pursued some form of continued study since leaving school; and

d   be recommended for such an award by an L.E.A., a Principal of an Establishment for Further Education, a Responsible Body or other approved person or body of persons.

A Mature Student's scholarship is tenable at a University or Polytechnic in the United Kingdom for a course of study approved by the Minister. The course must normally be one leading to an Honours degree. Scholarships are awarded for liberal studies only.

Mature Student scholarship grants are subject to a means test. There is no fixed emolument, but the Minister will have regard to the standard grant for maintenance at the university attended, any other award held by the scholar, and the scholar's private means.

Milk and Meals

Every local education authority must establish a school meals service and employ an organizer of school meals.

The meals service is to be available to day pupils at all schools maintained by the authority, which must provide, or secure the provision of, all the facilities and materials required for its maintenance. The managers or governors of every maintained school must afford all necessary facilities and make any necessary alterations to premises.

The authority must provide on all school days substantial mid-day meals and not less than one-third of a pint of milk a pupil for drinking; and may provide other meals and refreshments on school days, and milk, meals, and refreshments upon any other days.

The mid-day meals must be adequate in quantity and quality to serve as the main meal of the day, and the dietary suitably varied and nutritionally balanced.

The source and quality of the milk must be approved by the medical officer of health for the authority. If liquid milk of satisfactory standard is not available, the Minister may approve the substitution of full-cream milk suitably prepared for drinking, or of milk in the form of milk tablets.

In Circular 34 the Minister stated that he regarded it as important that as many children as possible should have two thirds of a pint of milk daily. In 1946 this had to be restricted to priority cases. As supplies of milk improved and rationing was abandoned this restriction was relaxed; but in 1956 it was reimposed except for delicate pupils in special schools.

Parents of pupils at special schools may be charged for meals and refreshments by a local authority, but no charge is to exceed the cost of the food or drink supplied. Parents of all other pupils are also charged, according to an approved rate for dinners, and for other meals or refreshments such sums as the local authority estimate will cover their cost, including overhead costs. Charges may be wholly or partially remitted in cases of financial hardship; determination of hardship rests in the first instance with the local authority. Sums payable by parents may be recovered summarily as a civil debt.

Charges to parents will continue until such time as sufficient canteens are established.[1] The same income scales for the remission of charges should obtain in all schools, at least up to the age at which attendance ceases to be compulsory. Prices have steadily risen; in 1951 the charge for school dinners was raised from 5*d.* to 7*d.*, in 1953 to 9*d.*, in 1956 to 10*d.*, in 1957 to 1*s.*, and in 1967 to 1*s.* 6*d.*

Free Milk

On and after 6 August 1946 milk for drinking supplied by local education authorities to pupils in attendance at maintained schools was made free of any charge to the parents of such pupils, provided that so much of the milk so supplied to boarders need be supplied free of charge to their parents as is obtained for such pupils by the authorities under arrangements for the provision of free milk to school pupils.

If any pupil avails himself so rarely or irregularly of the school meals service that waste or undue expense is involved, the authority may exclude him from its benefits.

Teachers' Supervision Duties

The authority must employ a suitable and adequate staff other than teachers for the preparation, cooking, service and, where necessary, transport of meals, and for washing up and other incidental matters; and, having regard to the authority's power to require teachers to supervise pupils, for supervising pupils at meals to such extent as may be needed.

No service by way of supervision shall be required of any teacher, and no voluntary assistance to the school meals service

---

[1] There were by the 1960s sufficient canteens, but charges will continue unless current government policy changes.

shall be given by any teacher, if, in the opinion of the authority, it would adversely affect the quality of the teaching given by that teacher. No teacher of any school shall be required to perform any service of supervision unless pupils from that school are included among the pupils supervised by the teacher. Otherwise, the authority may require teachers of any school to supervise pupils at dinner on school days; and in nursery schools or classes teachers may also be required to supervise other meals.

Educational Conferences

A local education authority may incur expenditure for the purpose of organizing or participating in the organization of conferences. Restrictions formerly imposed by the Minister of Education on the amount of expenditure were removed by *The Educational Conferences (Revocation) Regulations, 1959*, which came into operation on 1 April 1959.

An authority may pay or contribute towards yearly subscriptions to associations or other bodies whose functions involve the regular discussion of questions relating to education.

General Grants

In accordance with the Local Government Act, 1958, percentage grants from the Minister of Education to local education authorities were (with some exceptions, of which the School Milk and Meals Service was one) replaced, from 1 April 1959, by a system of General Grants (commonly known as 'block grants') from the Minister of Housing and Local Government to the County and County Borough Councils. These general grants are in respect of almost all the expenditure incurred by these authorities in providing public services, including education, in their areas; the idea behind their introduction was stated to be to give local authorities more freedom in expending the financial resources at their command. The introduction of 'block grants' was strongly opposed by the great majority of people professionally engaged in the public service of education, principally on the grounds that education, since it accounted for by far the greatest amount of the moneys expended by local authorities,[1] was therefore most liable

---

[1] Stated by the General Secretary of the Association of Education Committee (*Education*, 25 April 1958) to be 87·5 per cent.

to be 'raided' in order to pay for other local authority projects or to lower the local rates.

Percentage grants were made annually. The first General grant, made in 1959, was to cover two years; and succeeding grants have been made for the same period. In respect of the bulk of local authority expenditure on public education the Minister of Education presents an estimate, based on estimates submitted to him by the individual local education authorities, to the Minister of Housing and Local Government, who incorporates this into his total estimate for the General grant to be submitted to the Treasury.

Expenditure on teacher training, advanced further education and the education of pupils who do not belong to the area of any local authority is pooled among all the local authorities; for details see *The General Grants (Pooling Arrangements) Regulations, 1959.*

Education of Handicapped Pupils

The Handicapped Pupils and Special School Regulations, 1959, define the categories of pupils handicapped by physical or mental defect for whom authorities are required to provide special educational treatment as follows:

a   *Blind Pupils.* Pupils who have no sight or whose sight is or is likely to become so defective that they require education by methods not involving the use of sight.

b   *Partially Sighted Pupils.* Pupils who by reason of defective vision cannot follow the normal régime of ordinary schools without detriment to their sight or to their educational development, but can be educated by special methods involving the use of sight.

c   *Deaf Pupils.* Pupils who have no hearing or whose hearing is so defective that they require education by methods used for deaf pupils without naturally acquired speech or language.

d   *Partially Deaf*[1] *Pupils.* Pupils with naturally acquired speech and language whose hearing is so defective that they require for their education special arrangements or facilities though not necessarily all the educational methods used for deaf pupils.

e   *Educationally Sub-Normal Pupils.* Pupils who, by reason of limited ability or other conditions resulting in educational retardation,

---

[1] Since renamed 'partially hearing'.

require some specialized form of education wholly or partly in substitution for the education normally given in ordinary schools.

f   *Epileptic Pupils.* Pupils who by reason of epilepsy cannot be educated under the normal régime of ordinary schools without detriment to the interests of themselves or other pupils.

g   *Maladjusted Pupils.* Pupils who show evidence of emotional instability or psychological disturbance and require special educational treatment in order to effect their personal, social, or educational readjustment.

h   *Physically Handicapped Pupils.* Pupils not suffering solely from a defect of sight or hearing who by reason of disease or crippling defect cannot, without detriment to their health or educational development, be satisfactorily educated under the normal régime of ordinary schools.

i   *Pupils Suffering from Speech Defect.* Pupils who on account of defect or lack of speech not due to deafness require special educational treatment.

j   *Delicate Pupils.* Pupils not in any other category who by reason of impaired physical condition need a change of environment or cannot, without risk to their health or educational development, be educated under the normal régime of an ordinary school.

The regulations about admission, sessions, and employment of teachers are similar to those for normal schools. Teachers of blind, deaf or partially hearing children must possess special qualifications.

For handicapped children the maximum sizes of classes are: deaf, partially hearing, or suffering from speech defect, 10; blind and partially sighted, 15; maladjusted, 15; educationally sub-normal, epileptic, or physically handicapped, 20; delicate, 30.

An authority may not without the approval of the Minister provide new premises for a boarding home for handicapped pupils or alter existing premises. The Minister may make both capital and maintenance grants in respect of boarding homes conducted by persons other than the authority. Both maintained and voluntary boarding homes are open to inspection by H.M. Inspectors or other persons appointed by the Minister of Education. The authority is responsible for the medical and dental care of children in maintained and non-maintained boarding homes and boarded with foster parents.

School Health Service

Every authority must establish for their area a School Health Service and appoint a Principal School Medical Officer and a Principal School Dental Officer. The latter is responsible to the former for the School Dental Service. Every school nurse employed by the authority must, unless employed solely in a school clinic or on specialist duties, be qualified as a health visitor.

Every authority must keep medical and dental records, in a form approved by the Minister of Education, for every pupil attending a school maintained by them.

So far as is practicable, parents of day pupils must be given opportunity to be present at every medical and the first dental inspection of the children.

Further Education

The regulations about suitability of premises, precautions against fire and other dangers, including radioactive equipment and materials, efficiency of instruction, admission to and exclusion from courses, and employment of teachers, are generally similar to those for schools.

An authority may not without the approval of the Minister of Education provide new premises for a Further Education establishment, alter existing premises, purchase any article of equipment costing £500 or more, or articles for the initial furnishing and equipment of residential accommodation for students.

For a maintained technical or commercial college, school or college of art, farm institute, or residential college of adult education the authority must constitute a governing body, to be responsible to it for the conduct of the establishment. In the cases of the first four of these types of establishments (technical, commercial, art, farm) there must be substantial representation on the governing body of industrial, commercial and other appropriate interests, including, if approved advanced studies are being pursued, universities and professional bodies. These last must also be represented on the governing bodies of residential adult education colleges.

The Minister may make capital and maintenance grants in aid of facilities for further education provided by bodies other than local education authorities. The regulations for such facilities in respect of premises, equipment, admission and exclusion of students, employment of teachers, and inspection are similar to those for maintained establishments. The Minister of Education must approve all courses and arrangements for the charging of fees. No courses in religious subjects distinctive of any particular religious denomination may be included in the general programme of full-time instruction.

Among the bodies to whom the Minister of Education may pay grants are those officially known as 'Responsible Bodies'.

A Responsible Body is a body of persons, not being a local education authority or body exercising powers on behalf of such an authority, who are responsible for the provision of liberal education for adults.

To be eligible for recognition, a Responsible Body shall be—

a   A university (which may act through a committee, or a joint committee also representing other bodies); or
b   A national association or a district committee of a national association, having as one of its principal objects the promotion of liberal education for adults;
c   A joint body approved by the Minister and consisting of representatives of universities, national associations and local education authorities.

Training of Teachers

The Training of Teachers Regulations, 1967, which came into operation on 6 June 1967, combined in one instrument the provisions of *The Training of Teachers (Local Education Authorities) Regulations, 1959*, and *The Training of Teachers (Grant) Regulations, 1959*—which had reference to colleges and other establishments, including University Departments of Education, maintained by bodies other than Local Education Authorities—and incorporated the amendments subsequently made to these bodies of Regulations. They also introduced several important changes, including in particular a requirement (Regulation 12) that—

Every college shall be conducted in accordance with articles of government made with the approval of the Secretary of State, which shall in particular determine the functions to be exercised in relation to the college by the body providing the college, the governing body, the academic board and the principal.

The name 'training college' has disappeared. It is replaced by 'college of education'.

A local education authority may not without the approval of the Secretary of State, given after consultation with the Area Training Organization (A.T.O.) concerned, provide or maintain a training establishment.

The provisions relating to the reasonable exercise of functions, the making of reports and returns, and inspection contained in the Education Act, 1944, apply equally to L.E.A. and voluntary colleges.

The governing body of a voluntary college may not, in the selection of candidates for one half of the places, reject the application of a candidate on the ground of his religious faith; and,
No student may be required, as a condition of entering or remaining in a voluntary college, to comply with any rule of the college as to attendance at religious worship, observance or instruction if he claims exemption on the grounds that he does not belong to the denomination of the college.

A student is not eligible for admission to a college of education or a department of education unless he is at least 18 years of age (on 1 October for a course beginning in the autumn). For admission to a college of education (technical) he must be at least 24.

A student may not be admitted to an establishment for a course of initial training unless the body providing the establishment is satisfied as to his good character and health, his physical capacity for teaching and his suitability for the teaching profession in other respects.

A student shall not without the approval of the A.T.O. concerned be eligible for admission to a training establishment unless he holds the required minimum academic qualifications. These, which are different for colleges of education, colleges of education (technical), art training centres, and departments of education, are set out in Schedule 2 of the Regulations.

A 'recognised student' means a person eligible for grant in accordance with arrangements approved by the Secretary of State under
section 2(3) of the Education Act, 1962.

A teacher, not being an occasional teacher, shall be employed:
a   in a voluntary college, under a written agreement;
b   in a maintained college, under a written agreement or a minute of
     the authority appointing him to a post specified in the agreement
     or minute.

The Secretary of State may pay grants to the governing body
of any voluntary institution which provides courses for or is
otherwise concerned with the training of teachers. He may make
loans to the governing body of any voluntary college of education. He may pay grants to persons undergoing training as teachers.

Since 1955 it has no longer been required that a recognized
student sign a declaration of intention to teach in a grant-aided
school.

The Training of Teachers (Local Education Authorities) Amending Regulations, 1960 (S.I. 1960/708) extended the length of an
initial teachers' training course for students without university
degrees (except at technical training colleges and art centres) from
two to three years as from 1 September 1960. It gave Area Training Organizations power to sanction shorter courses of one or two
years' duration if the age, education and experience of a student
justifies it.

Independent Schools

Every application by a proprietor for the registration of his
independent school must be made in writing, addressed to the
Registrar of Independent Schools, Department of Education and
Science, Curzon Street, London, W.1, and must contain the
particulars specified in a Schedule to The Independent Schools Registration Regulations, 1957 (S.I. 1957/929).

Each January proprietors must send in writing to the Registrar particulars of any changes in (a) the number of pupils by sex
and age groups, (b) the number of boarders, if any, by sex groups,
and (c) the teaching staff.

A school which has received from the Minister notification
that he recognizes it as efficient is exempt from registration under
Section 70 of the Education Act, 1944.

Some Important Circulars

The following are among the more important Circulars issued by the Ministry of Education between August 1944 and March 1964, and by the Department of Education and Science from April 1964 to September 1967. Copies are available from H.M.S.O.

NOTE.—Many of the Circulars listed here have been cancelled by later ones, but they are retained for their historical interest.

No.	Date	Title	Contents
1	15.viii.44	The Education Act, 1944.	A statement of the Minister's intentions and requirements. Includes the postponement of the raising of the school age.
5	15.ix.44	Schemes of Divisional Administration.	General principles and guidance to local education authorities.
10	19.xi.44	Draft Building Regulations.	Explanatory of the Regulations. See also *Memorandum on the Building Regulations* (H.M.S.O.).
11	7.xi.44	Acquisition of Sites.	States that L.E.As. proposing immediate purchases must show that the sites are required to meet urgent needs within two years of the end of the European War; and that such acquisitions will be placed on the same footing as acquisitions for housing purposes.
13	10.xi.44	Leisure-time Provision for School Children.	Proposes the provision of facilities for children aged 11–14 comparable with those of the Youth Service.

No.	Date	Title	Contents
17	28.xi.44	National Camps.	States that some camps provided by the National Camps Corporation, which were used during the war to house evacuated schools, will shortly be available to L.E.As. for general education purposes.
18	19.xii.44	Emergency Recruitment and Training of Teachers.	Includes the report of the Minister's Advisory Committee on standards and methods of selection of candidates.
20	22.xii.44	Community Centres.	Their provision to be regarded as within the scope of L.E.As. This is not to preclude provision by other local authorities or voluntary bodies, to whom the Minister of Education will make direct grants in aid. See also the pamphlet *Community Centres* (H.M.S.O.), issued with this circular.
21	4.i.45	School Meals.	Need for the utmost expansion of the School Meals Service urged. After the repair of bomb-damaged houses, this service to be given priority equal to housing. In administering the service 'nothing must be done which will adversely affect the performance by teachers of their primary function of teaching.' See also Circular 34.
25	9.iii.45	Agricultural Education.	Issued jointly with the Ministry of Agriculture. Announces a new division of functions between the two ministries whereby the L.E.As. are to be responsible for agricultural education up to and including the Farm Institute level.
26	13.iii.45	Draft Regulations under Section 81. Scholarships and other benefits.	Explains and amplifies the Regulations, *q.v.* The L.E.As. are told to submit particulars of the arrangements they propose to make for exercising their powers under Section 81. Amounts and income levels are suggested for university awards.
28	8.v.45	Preparation of Development Plan.	Form in which plan is to be submitted: L.E.As. encouraged to submit plans by instalments.

No.	Date	Title	Contents
29	12.iii.45	School Medical Service.	General guidance to L.E.As. on interim arrangements pending the establishment of the National Health Service.
30	12.iii.45	Draft Regulations for Primary and Secondary Schools.	Explains and amplifies the Regulations, *q.v.* Contains defence of the decision to reduce primary classes only to 40.
32	16.iii.45	Direct Grant Grammar Schools.	Conditions of recognition and the procedure for applying for recognition. No grant allowed for preparatory departments.
34	27.iii.45	Draft Provision of Milk and Meals Regulations.	Explains and amplifies the Regulations, *q.v.* Emphasizes that while economy is essential this is not to mean poor quality or small quantity of food.
36	28.iii.45	Teachers (Superannuation) Act, 1945.	Notes on the changes effected by the Act.
37	23.iii.35	Draft Education (Local Education Authorities) Grant Regulations, 1945.	Notes on the Regulations, *q.v.*
41	18.iv.45	Handicapped Pupils and Medical Services Regulations, 1945.	Explains and amplifies the Regulations, *q.v.* Emphasizes the two new categories—maladjusted children and children with speech defects—and that provision is made in the Act for research.
49	30.v.45	Provision of Additional Training College Accommodation.	Invites proposals for the expansion of permanent colleges and the establishment of new ones.
50	24.v.45	National Camps.	Announces that more camps used during the war to house evacuated schools will shortly be available to L.E.As. for general educational purposes. See Circular 17.

No.	Date	Title	Contents
51	15.vi.45	Provision of facilities for Recreation and Social and Physical Training.	Alters the basis of grant-aid, which will in future be made directly by the Minister to headquarters of national voluntary organizations. Other grant-aid to be made by L.E.As.
51	18.viii.48	Addendum.	Aid for Village Halls.
53	22.vi.45	Courses of Training for those engaging in the Youth Service.	Notes on one-year full-time courses at universities, and part-time courses.
55	5.vii.45	Training of Technical Teachers.	Announces that this is to be incorporated in the Emergency Scheme of Training for Teachers.
56	9.vii.45	Further Education. Some immediate problems.	States that the need for buildings is very urgent, urges co-operation with industry in respect of staff and accommodation, and advises on the types of teacher to recruit.
57	9.vii.45	Demobilization and Adult Education.	Emphasizes what Services' education has done, suggests that this presents 'a new problem and a new opportunity', and urges the need for 'less formal educational activities'.
59	14.vii.45	The Training of Nursery Students in Nurseries, Nursery Schools, and Nursery Classes.	Joint circular with Ministry of Health 126/45. Announces the institution of a National Nursery Certificate.
61	9.viii.45	Revised Regulations for Further Education.	Explains and amplifies the Regulations (q.v.) which bring Further Education and Adult Education into one body of Regulations.
64	27.ix.45	Raising the Compulsory School Age.	Announces the postponement of the raising of the age to 15 to 1 April 1947.
65	2.xi.45	Road Safety among School Children.	Includes Ministry of War Transport Circular 588.
66	12.xi.45	Qualifications of Teachers in Special Schools.	Gives the conditions for recognition as qualified teachers.

No.	Date	Title	Contents
66	10.i.49	Addendum.	Long service qualification.
68	12.xi.45	Training of Disabled Persons.	Shared between Ministries of Education and Labour.
69	20.xi.45	Franco-British understanding through the Schools.	Suggests its development by (a) correspondence between schools, and (b) 'linking' of a British with a French school for a variety of activities, including visits. See also Circular 118.
73	12.xii.45	Organization of Secondary Schools.	Suggests to L.E.As. that they should plan for approximately 70–75 per cent. of pupils in Modern Schools, 25–30 per cent. in Grammar and Technical. Adds that it is 'not contemplated that this separate classification of schools will be irrevocable'.
75	14.xii.45	Nursery Provision for Children under 5.	Joint Circular with Ministry of Health. Advocates the joint planning of educational and welfare facilities. L.E.As. asked to review their wartime nurseries to see which should be taken over by the welfare authority or the L.E.A., which turned into nursery schools, and which closed.
77	13.xii.45	Emergency Training of Teachers.	Announces a target of 12,000 teachers in training by the end of 1946, and solicits the aid of L.E.As. in providing accommodation.
79	1.i.46	Boarding School Provision for Educationally Subnormal and Maladjusted Children.	Stresses the serious inadequacy of such provision and urges that 'every expedient' be used to expand it.
83	14.i.46	Choice of Schools.	A statement of the principles to be applied by L.E.As. to give parents an effective choice of county and voluntary schools, with special reference to (a) choice for religious reasons, (b) schools outside the area in which parents live, and (c) boarding schools.

No.	Date	Title	Contents
85	12.ii.46	Revised Regulations for the Training of Teachers.	See the Regulations, which make all L.E.As. share the expense of the provision of training facilities.
87	20.ii.46	Regional Organization of Further Education.	L.E.As. asked to consider Regional Advisory Councils and to set up at once Regional Academic Boards of Technology.
89	11.iii.46	Voluntary Secondary Schools.	Position clarified.
90	8.iii.46	Development Plans.	Grants extension of time for submission of up to three months. Also discusses policy regarding secondary schools, village schools, and boarding schools.
91	2.v.46	Recognition of Schools and other Educational Establishments as Efficient.	Includes Rules 16, which state the conditions of recognition, revised to take account of the Education Act, 1944, and the Teachers (Superannuation) Act, 1945.
94	8.iv.46	Research in Technical Colleges.	Stresses its value, states that the present amount is small, and suggests that applied rather than fundamental research is appropriate.
95	28.iii.46	Teachers' Superannuation.	See S.R. & O. 415 of 1946, which gives new scheme for schools not grant-aided.
96	28.iii.46	School Meals Service.	Announces that milk will be made free in August 1946, meals as soon as canteen facilities equal the demand.
97	12.iv.46	School Meals and Midday Supervision.	Gives the compromise arrived at between the Ministry and the teachers' associations about supervision; and discusses the problems raised in some detail. See also Circulars 21, 34 and 349.
98	10.iv.46	The Status of Technical, Commercial and Art Colleges.	Various proposals for raising the status of major colleges.
104	16.v.46	Awards for University Students.	Explanatory of the Regulations, q.v.

No.	Date	Title	Contents
111	24.v.46	The Education Act, 1946.	Underlines points of particular interest to L.E.As. See Appendix III.
112	11.vi.46	Organization of the Training of Teachers.	Accepts the fact that universities will differ in the arrangements they make.
113	26.vi.46	Secondary School Examinations Council.	Announces that the Minister will take over full responsibility for the direction of policy and the general arrangement of external examinations for secondary schools; and the reconstruction of the S.S.E.C.
114	16.vii.46	Special Courses for Uncertificated Teachers.	To start Autumn 1947, one-year courses leading to the award of the Teacher's Certificate.
118	9.vii.46	Supplement to Circular 69.	Extends the scheme to Belgium.
119	22.vii.46	The Milk in Schools Scheme.	Main principles and arrangements for the provision of free milk.
120	19.viii.46	Boarding Education.	Progressive development urged. A committee set up to facilitate. See also Circular 90.
123	28.viii.46	The Relations between L.E.As. and the National Agricultural Advisory Service.	Joint circular with the Ministry of Agriculture. Defines responsibilities preparatory to N.A.A.S. coming into being (on 1.x.46). See also Circular 25.
127	14.x.46	United Nations Educational, Scientific and Cultural Organization.	Suggests 'Unesco Week' in schools while Conference sitting. Announces publications on Unesco.
129	9.i.47	Family Allowances.	Children above compulsory school age.
133	19.iii.47	Schemes of Further Education and Plans for County Colleges.	Includes Ministry of Education Pamphlet No. 8, Further Education.
134	19.xii.46	The Educational Building Programme 1947.	£24m. to be spent. Categories of projects.

No.	Date	Title	Contents
136	18.iii.47	Approval of Graduates as Qualified Teachers.	Excludes graduates who have failed an approved course of professional training.
140	25.iv.47	Secular Instruction elsewhere than on the school premises.	H.M.I.'s consent no longer needed. Draft Regulations attached.
144	16.vi.47	Organization of Secondary Education.	Defines bilateral, multilateral and comprehensive schools.
151	18.vii.47	School Records of Individual Development.	What they should contain.
156	6.xi.47	Distribution of Grants to L.E.As.	Includes the revised Main Grant formula.
160	29.i.48	Training of Staff for Child Guidance.	Measures to encourage this.
161	1.iii.48	Grants for Agricultural Education provided by L.E.As.	Joint Circular with Ministry of Agriculture No. 4 of 1948.
162	3.iii.48	Correspondence with German schools.	Modern Language Association scheme.
168	23.iv.48	Examinations in Secondary Schools.	Report of the Secondary Schools Examination Council.
170	26.v.48	Secondment of Teachers for Overseas Service.	Includes form of application.
173	21.vi.48	Qualified Teachers and Temporary Teachers.	Restates Circular 30 and defines policy more precisely.
174	16.vi.48	Supply and Employment of Teachers for Primary and Secondary Schools.	Estimates of numbers in the succeeding five years.
177	30.vi.48	The Education (Miscellaneous Provisions) Act, 1948.	Deals with those provisions of the Act which specially affect current administration.
179	4.viii.48	The School Health Service and Handicapped Pupils.	Effect of the establishment of the National Health Service.

No.	Date	Title	Contents
199	29.iii.49	Royal College of Art.	Includes prospectus of the reorganized college.
201	12.iv.49	Two-year part-time study of teachers trained in Emergency Colleges.	Suggestions for improvement, and revised grant arrangements.
205	6.ix.49	Examinations in Secondary Schools.	S.S.E.C. recommendations on objective tests and internal examinations accepted.
208	1.ii.50	Local Government Manpower Committee.	Includes copy of its report.
209	28.x.49	Capital Investment in 1950.	Priorities in educational building.
210	12.vii.50	Expenditure of L.E.As.	Economies suggested.
213	6.iii.50	Minimum examination qualifications for candidates seeking admission to training colleges.	Explained by title.
221	19.vi.50	L.E.A. awards at Universities and University Colleges.	Deprecates division of awards into major and minor, and condemns loans.
224	14.viii.50	Teachers' Superannuation Acts.	Defines full-time service.
227	28.ix.50	Professional Bodies' requirements in terms of the General Certificate of Education.	The first list. Revised in 1952 and 1955. Superseded in 1958 by Circular 338. List periodically revised since.
230	19.xii.50	Training of Technical Teachers.	The three Emergency Colleges to be included in the general national system.
234	1.iii.51	University Awards.	Abolishes the four-year grant to intending teachers.
240	5.x.51	Regulations prescribing standards for school premises.	Requirements reduced and more scope for variety allowed.

No.	Date	Title	Contents
242	7.xii.51	Educational Expenditure.	An aggregate cut of 5 per cent. on forecasts for 1952–53 called for.
245	4.ii.52	Capital Investment in 1952.	Educational building programmes for 1951–52 and 1952–53 telescoped. Priorities defined.
248	28.iii.52	Protection of School Children against Tuberculosis.	Precautions that may be taken in schools.
249	28.iii.52	Medical Examination of Entrants to Teacher Training and Teaching.	To be undertaken by School Medical Officers. Guidance on medical standards attached.
250	18.iv.52	Organization of the School Meals Service.	L.E.As. to review with the object of reducing overhead costs.
254	30.vi.52	National Health Service and School Health Service.	Joint circular with Ministry of Health 22/52. Urges health and education authorities to build up dental staffs to meet the needs of children and mothers.
255	14.vii.62	Advanced Technology.	Announces 75 per cent. grant for advanced technological study and research in technical colleges.
256	4.ix.52	Examinations in Secondary Schools.	Defines nature and purpose of the General Certificate of Education examination.
262	22.i.53	School Meals Service.	Cost of school dinners raised to 9d. as from 1 March 1953.
263	2.iii.53	Selection for L.E.A. awards at Universities.	Includes agreed statement by universities, Ministry, and L.E.As. No more formal recommendations by universities.
264	10.iii.53	Educational Building.	Basic limits of cost per place to be adjusted periodically in step with index of building costs.
265	20.vii.53	Juvenile Delinquency.	Joint circular with Home Office 99/1953. Suggestions made by committees set up after 1949 appeal to civic dignitaries.
268	17.viii.53	Education (Miscellaneous Provisions) Act, 1953.	Draws attention to principal features. See also Appendix v.

No.	Date	Title	Contents
269	25.viii.53	The School Health Service and Handicapped Pupils Regulations, 1953.	Describes and explains the principal changes in the Regulations, *q.v.*
272	15.i.54	Prevention of Food Poisoning in School Canteens.	Possible risks and measures to avoid them.
273	23.iv.54	The Standards for School Premises Regulations, 1954.	See the Regulations. This Circular cancels No. 240.
274	23.iv.54	Educational Building.	Alterations in the formula for calculating limits of net cost, consequent upon changes made in the Standards for School Premises Regulations, 1954.
276	25.vi.54	Provision of Special Schools.	Proposes review of present position and future plans. Lays down the principle that: 'No handicapped pupil should be sent to a special school who can be satisfactorily educated in an ordinary school.'
278	1.vii.54	Milk-in-Schools Scheme.	L.E.As. to take over from the Ministry of Food responsibility to provide milk for pupils at maintained schools.
280	28.viii.54	Reduction in Overlarge Classes.	Admission of children under 5 to be restricted or prohibited if it stands in the way of reducing the size of classes.
283	3.xii.54	Educational Building.	Supersedes Circular 245. Action to be begun at once to reorganize all rural schools. Control over amounts spent on minor projects abolished, and limit for individual projects raised to £10,000. Restrictions removed on building for Further Education.
284	19.iv.55	Qualified Teachers and Temporary Teachers.	Current policy about qualifications and status. Supersedes Circulars 136 and 173.
	1.x.56	——	More 'graduate-equivalents' listed.

No.	Date	Title	Contents
286	24.v.55	Grants to Training College Students.	Accepts working party's report (same title, H.M.S.O., Standard rates, and uniform scale for assessing personal grants.
289	9.vii.55	Examinations in Secondary Schools.	Existing G.C.E. standards to be maintained; no new examinations.
290	5.viii.55	School Meals Services.	Defines nutritional standards for school dinners.
301	26.iv.56	Educational Building.	Despite increased building costs limits for new schools unchanged.
304	6.vi.56	Expenditure on Furniture and Equipment.	Cost limits fixed for schools.
305	21.vi.56	Organization of Technical Colleges.	To be in four grades: local, area, regional, advanced technology; conditions for recognizing last.
306	16.vi.56	Educational Buildings.	Starting dates for 1956–7 school projects deferred.
307	27.vi.56	Fees for Further Education.	To be substantially increased from September 1956.
308	27.vi.56	School Meals Service	Dinner charge raised to 10d., day special schools alone excepted.
310	4.ix.56	Teachers' (Superannuation) Act, 1956.	Draws attention to provisions requiring early action by employers.
312	11.ix.56	The Education of Patients in Hospital.	Present position, arrangements, methods, problems.
313	18.ix.56	School Staffing and Reduction of Overlarge classes.	Close adherence to the policy set out in Circular 280 still necessary.
315	2.xi.56	Awards for post-graduate study.	D.S.I.R. to continue to award these in science and technology, but in greater number. The Ministry of Education to award 'State Studentships' in arts subjects.
318	5.xii.56	Employment and Distribution of Teachers.	L.E.As. urged to help hard-pressed areas by working voluntary 'Quota' scheme—since periodically revised.
319	7.i.57	Reopening of the Direct Grant List.	Conditions of application.
320	1.iii.57	Hostels at Technical Colleges.	Need for more. Suggested scale of provision, and of accommodation.

No.	Date	Title	Contents
322	12.iv.57	Libraries in Technical Colleges.	Importance stressed. Notes on functions, contents and accommodation.
323	13.v.57	Liberal Education in Technical Colleges.	Ways to secure it.
325	17.vi.57	Three-year Training Course for Teachers.	Gives Government's decision to introduce this in September 1960.
326	3.vii.57	Examinations in Secondary Schools.	No change in G.C.E. Regionally organized examinations permitted for pupils aged 16 and upwards.
327	13.vii.57	Educational Maintenance Allowances for pupils over compulsory school age.	Revised scales set out.
330	25.x.57	Teaching Service and the teaching of English overseas.	Ministry of Education to set up unit to recruit teachers and place on return.
332	8.i.58	Welfare of Overseas students in technical colleges.	Suggestions to colleges for its improvement.
336	12.ii.58	Recruitment of Teachers for Technical Colleges.	7,000 full-time and 8,000 part-time more wanted by 1960–61.
340	14.vii.58	Art Education.	National Advisory Council set up. Ministry of Education to cease conducting art examinations.
342	3.xii.58	Educational Building.	Plans for a five-year programme.
344	17.xii.58	Divisional Administration in Excepted Districts.	Suggestions for a review of powers, with the possibility of enlarging them.
346	25.ii.59	Agricultural Education.	Some new responsibilities given to Ministry of Education.
347	10.iii.59	Child Guidance.	Suggestions for developing the Service.
349	20.iii.59	The School Meals Service and the Teacher.	Suggestions for reducing the teacher's burden. Cancels Circular 97.

No.	Date	Title	Contents
350	24.iii.59	Local Government Act, 1958.	Changes in administrative procedure resulting from the introduction of general grants.
351	24.iii.59	The Further Education (Local Education Authorities) Regulations, 1959.	Comments upon various new regulations.
352	24.iii.59	School Health Service, Medical Examinations, Handicapped Pupils, Handicapped Pupils (Boarding) and Special Schools and Establishments (Grants) Regulations, 1959.	Comment and explanation on these new Bodies of Regulations.
353	24.iii.59	The School Meals Service: Finance.	Changes due to the introduction of general grants.
354	24.iii.59	The Training of Teachers (Local Education Authorities) Regulations, 1959, and The Training of Teachers (Grant) Regulations, 1959.	Comment and explanation on these new bodies of Regulations.

NOTE.—From April 1959 a new style of numbering was adopted.

No.	Date	Title	Contents
1/59	13.iv.59	Technical Education: The Next Step.	Between 1961–64 £15m. a year to be spent on buildings and £9m. on equipment.
2/59	27.iv.59	Teaching about the Commonwealth.	Advice and help for teachers.
3/59	26.v.59	The Standards of School Premises Regulations, 1959.	Comment and explanation on changes in the Regulations.
5/59	11.vi.59	Further Education for Commerce.	A large development urged along the lines proposed by the Advisory Committee.
7/59	10.viii.59	Governing Bodies for Major Establishments of Further Education.	All to have them, with large representation of industry and commerce.

No.	Date	Title	Contents
10/59	3.ix.59	The Remodelling of Old Schools.	L.E.As. urged to prepare schemes for urgent projects.
11/59	30.ix.59	The Schools and International Affairs.	Sources of information about the United Nations.
2/60	1.iii.60	Land Questions.	Explains Town and Country Planning Act, 1959.
6/60	13.iv.60	Educational Building.	Procedures streamlined. Cost limits raised 10 per cent. for secondary and 6 per cent. for primary schools.
	1.iii.61	(Addendum 1)	Nett costs raised.
7/60	24.v.60	Further Education for Agriculture.	Minister accepts de la Warr Report.
8/60	31.v.60	Nursery Education.	No expansion.
9/60	29.vi.60	The Education Service and Training for Industry.	Advocates extended courses in secondary schools, full-time courses in technical colleges, and integration of education and apprentice training.
5/61	28.iii.61	University and Comparable awards.	New scale of grants and parental contributions.
7/61	1.v.61	Training of Teachers.	New scale of grants. Minister appoints Standing Advisory Committee on awards, including training college grants.
9/61	12.v.61	Changes in the G.C.E. Advanced Level Examination.	Scheme of graded passes from 1963.
11/61	3.vii.61	Special Educational Treatment for ESN pupils.	Review of progress and practice.
13/61	28.vii.61	Educational Building.	Reduction in minor works programme. Priority increased for science and technical building projects.
14/61	18.ix.61	Young children handicapped by impaired hearing.	Importance of early diagnosis. Joint Circular with Ministry of Health 23/61.
7/62	10.viii.62	Training of Teachers.	New scale of grants, superseding that of 7/61.
9/62	24.x.62	Awards for first degree and comparable courses.	Duty laid on L.E.As. by the Education Act, 1962.
12/62	29.xi.62	The Youth Service.	Training of part-time leaders.

No.	Date	Title	Contents
5/63	5.iv.63	The School Dinner and Midday Supervision.	Additional and supervisory staff: voluntary assistance by teachers.
9/63	23.v.63	The Certificate of Secondary Education.	Conditions of recognition.
8/63	27.v.63	Grants to Students.	Co-operation between England, Scotland and Northern Ireland.
13/63	20.xii.63	Employment and Distribution of Teachers.	Quota continued. Married women returners exempt for two years.
1/64	28.ii.64	Industrialized Building and Educational Building Consortia.	Gives particulars of the existing five Consortia.
5/64	31.iii.64	Awards for Post-graduate study.	Five types of awards. Supersedes Circular 315.
9/64	23.vii.64	Remission of the School Dinner charge.	National Scale introduced.
13/64	29.ix.64	The Schools Council for the Curriculum and Examinations.	Definition of the Council's task.
14/64	6.x.64	The Henniker Heaton Report on Day Release.	Endorsement by the Secretary of of State.
1/65	1.i.65	Employment and Distribution of Teachers.	Quota slightly reduced but more off-quota teachers allowed.
2/65	29.i.65	The School Dinner and Mid-day Supervision.	Clarifies the position about teacher's voluntary aid.
5/65	30.iv.65	Awards for Post-graduate Study.	Changes in arts and social studies. Supersedes 5/64.
6/65	18.v.65	Part-time Teaching in the schools.	Sixfold increase in 10 years; more needed.
7/65	14.vi.65	The Education of Immigrants.	Problems, advice and assistance.
8/65	24.vi.65	A Policy for the Arts.	Summarizes White Paper (Cd. 2601, same title). Joint with 53/65, Ministry of Housing and Local Government.

No.	Date	Title	Contents
10/65	12.vii.65	The Organization of Secondary Education.	L.E.As. 'requested' to submit plans for reorganizing secondary education on comprehensive lines. Six main forms described.
12/65	24.viii.65	Deferment of Capital Expenditure.	How 6 months' pause will affect education service.
3/66	26.i.66	The Nutritional Standard of School Dinners..	More meat less often; more of other protein foods. Supersedes Circular 290.
7/66	3.iii.66	Courses of Further Training for Teachers in Further Education.	More needed. Not to be restricted to qualified teachers.
8/66	24.v.66	A Plan for Polytechnics and Other Colleges.	Attached to copy of White Paper bearing same title.
9/66	31.iii.66	Co-ordination of Education, Health and Welfare Services for Handicapped Children and Young People.	Joint with 7/66 of Ministry of Health. Urges review, especially of aspects of common concern.
10/66	10.iii.66	School Building Programmes: Major and Minor 1967/68—1969/70.	Priorities to projects for children otherwise without school. No new secondary projects not on comprehensive lines.
11/66	12.iv.66	Technical College Resources: Size of Classes and Approval of F.E. courses.	New minimum class sizes specified for full and part-time courses.
17/66	29.vi.66	The National Insurance Act, 1966.	Additional contribution towards new benefits.
18/66	9.ix.66	Training of Teachers. Grants to recognized students at Teacher Training Establishments.	Consolidated arrangements covering colleges, U.D.Es., art training centres, Institutes of Education. Includes B.Ed.
20/66	5.ix.66	School Meals Service Technical Advice and Inspection.	H.M.I. replaced by professional catering experts.
21/66	13.ix.66	Training of Teachers for Further Education.	Minister rejects proposal for compulsory training.

No.	Date	Title	Contents
24/66	13.xii.66	Relations between Colleges of Education and Schools: Teaching Practice.	Information and advice. Longer periods of practice urged.
27/66	21.xii.66	Fees for Students from outside the United Kingdom attending full-time and sandwich courses in establishments of further education.	To be substantially increased from the 1967–68 session.
1/67	10.i.67	Employment and Distribution of Teachers.	During 1967, reduction of 0·4 per cent in quota.
2/67	7.ii.67	The Government of Colleges of Education.	To be reconstituted along lines of 'Weaver' Report.
3/67	22.iii.67	Education Act, 1967.	Explains the Act's three purposes.
4/67	5.vi.67	The Training of Teachers Regulations, 1967.	Explains these consolidated Regulations, q.v.
8/67	21.vii.67	Immigrants and the Youth Service.	Suggestions for action on report of same title.
11/67	24.viii.67	School Building in Educational Priority Areas.	Basis for allocating the £16m. over two years earmarked for this purpose.

The Education Act, 1946

THIS Act 'to amend and supplement the law relating to education' (and that about public libraries) received the Royal Assent on 22 May 1946. It contains 17 Sections and two Schedules.

Section 1 enables a local education authority, in stated circumstances, to pay the expenses of such enlargement of a controlled school as virtually amounts to the establishment of a new school.

Section 2 provides that where a school organized in two or more separate departments is to be divided into two or more separate schools, each of the schools shall retain the original status of county or voluntary.

Section 3 provides that in relation to the maintenance of voluntary schools the duties of local education authorities and managers and governors shall be performed in accordance with the provisions of the First Schedule of this Act, which alters Section 15 (3) of the 1944 Act.

Section 4 defines the expression 'school buildings' as 'any building or part of a building forming part of the school premises', except any required only—

a   as a caretaker's dwelling;
b   for use in connection with playing-fields;
c   for affording facilities for enabling the local education authorities to carry out their functions with respect to medical inspection or treatment; or
d   for affording facilities for providing milk, meals or other refreshment for pupils in attendance at the school.

The section provides that managers, governors or trustees of a voluntary school shall pay over to the local education authority any proceeds from the letting or hiring of any part of the school premises other than school buildings.

Section 5 amends Section 109 of the 1944 Act to enable local education authorities, in stated circumstances, to provide temporary accommodation for voluntary schools whether or not the permanent accommodation will be provided by the voluntary school authorities.

Section 6 enables a local education authority to execute any building work, repair work or similar work required for the purposes of a controlled school.

Section 7 makes it clear that the collective act of worship with which the school day in county and voluntary schools is required to begin must take place on the school premises; except that in aided and special agreement schools it may on special occasions take place elsewhere, provided due notice (normally not less than 14 days) be given to the parents.

Section 8 provides that a child or a young person under compulsion to attend a school or county college is deemed to have attained the 'leaving age' only at the end of a term.

Section 9 enables local education authorities to provide clothing free of charge and without inquiry into the parents' means for pupils attending maintained residential schools or educational institutions, nursery schools or classes.

Section 10 is of particular importance to teachers. It amends Section 94 of the Local Government Act, 1933, to provide that—

a person shall not, by reason of his being a teacher in, or being otherwise employed in, any school, college or other educational institution maintained or assisted by a local education authority, be disqualified for being a member of any committee or sub-committee of any local authority—

a   appointed for the purposes of the enactments relating to education;
b   appointed for the care of the mentally defective; or
c   appointed . . . for purposes connected with the execution of the Public Libraries Acts, 1892 to 1919.

Nor may anyone be disqualified because he is a teacher from being elected to a county district council.

Section 11 provides that a local education authority may defray the travelling expenses of members of divisional executives for journeys involving travel outside the area of a single county district. Such expenditure will not, however, rank for grant.

Section 12 secures compensation to officers of a county council who may suffer direct pecuniary loss through any of their functions being transferred to a divisional executive.

Section 13 provides that divisional executives may authorize their committees and sub-committees to exercise any functions which the executive is authorized to exercise on behalf of the L.E.A.; and that divisional executive documents shall be received in evidence.

Section 14 provides that the provisions of the 1944 Act specified in the Second Schedule of this Act shall have effect subject to the amendments there specified.

Section 15 provides that any increase in the Minister's expenditure under the Education Acts which is due to the passing of this Act shall be met by Parliament.

Section 16 is the interpretation section; it is noted here that the 'site' of a school does not include playing-fields.

Section 17 gives the title of the Act, and states that it does not extend to Scotland or Northern Ireland.

The Education (Miscellaneous Provisions) Act, 1948

THIS Act received the Royal Assent on 30 June 1948. It amends the Education Acts, 1944 and 1946, the Endowed Schools Acts, 1869 to 1908, the provisions of the Mental Deficiency Act, 1913, as to children incapable of receiving education, and the provision of the Children and Young Persons Act, 1933, as to the minimum age of employment. It contains 14 Sections and two Schedules.

Section 1 provides that powers formerly vested in the Charity Commissioners and later vested for the time being in the Minister of Education may by Order in Council be vested again in the Commissioners.

Section 2 extends the powers conferred by the Endowed Schools Acts, 1869 to 1908 (to alter, add to, and make new trusts for educational endowments, and to consolidate or divide endowments) to comprise endowments for any educational purpose.

E.A.—8

Previously these powers were confined to endowments for the purposes of educating boys and girls at school or for exhibitions.

No power is granted to alter an endowment which constitutes or forms part of the endowment of (*a*) a university, university college, or college of a university, and (*b*) a school not maintained by a local education authority.

Section 3 re-defines primary and secondary education, thus amending Section 8 (1) of the 1944 Act.

Primary education is defined as 'full-time education suitable to the requirements of junior pupils who have not attained the age of ten years and six months, and full-time education suitable to the requirements of junior pupils who have attained that age and whom it is expedient to educate together with junior pupils who have not attained that age.'

Reference to Section 114 of the 1944 Act will show that the upper limit of the age of junior pupils (i.e. 12) has not been altered.

To the definition of secondary education in Section 8 (1) (*b*) of the 1944 Act there are added the words: 'and full-time education suitable to the requirements of junior pupils who have attained the age of ten years and six months and whom it is expedient to educate together with senior pupils'. This Section was included to enable children of good intelligence and attainments to be promoted earlier to secondary schools.

Section 4 gives local education authorities powers to transfer pupils from maintained primary schools at this earlier age. It also states that, exceptional circumstances apart, there is no legal obligation upon the proprietor of a school to admit a child except at the beginning of a school term, nor upon a parent to cause his child to receive full-time education during any period when he cannot arrange for him to become a registered pupil at a school.

Section 5 provides that a local education authority may provide clothing for any pupil who is a boarder at any educational institution maintained by them, for any pupil in a nursery school or class maintained by them, and for any other pupil in a school maintained by them, including special schools, who appears to them unable because of the inadequacy or unsuitability of his clothing to take full advantage of the education provided at the school. With the consent of the proprietor, and upon agreed financial terms, the local education authority may secure clothing for such a child at a non-maintained school.

Section 6 provides that a local education authority shall be entitled to recoupment of the cost of educating pupils not belonging to their area. It defines what 'belonging to an area' means. Disputes about this are to be determined by the Minister.

Section 7 amends the powers of the Minister to modify his requirement of conformity to prescribed standards for school premises in cases where he considers it unreasonable to exact full conformity. The amendment deals particularly with awkward sites and temporary buildings.

Section 8 provides that if the local health authority thinks a decision that a child is incapable because of mental disability of being educated at school should be reviewed, they shall notify the local education authority. If after review it appears that the child is not so incapable the original report shall be cancelled.

Section 9 provides that when parents are prosecuted for failing to comply with a school attendance order, or to cause children to attend regularly at school, if the question arises, the child shall be presumed to have been of compulsory school age at the time of the offence unless the parent proves the contrary.

Section 10 clarifies the right of the local education authority to acquire land for educational purposes.

Section 11 provides that the provisions of the principal Acts specified in the following Schedules have effect subject to the amendments there detailed. Section 12 provides that Regulations made under this Act shall be made in the normal fashion. Section 13 deals similarly with any increase of expenditure due to the Act. Section 14 gives the citation of the Act, and states that it does not extend to Scotland or Northern Ireland.

The Schedules list the minor and consequential amendments.

The Education (Miscellaneous Provisions) Act, 1953

THIS Act received the Royal Assent on 14 July 1953. It amends the Education Act, 1944, and the Education (Miscellaneous Provisions) Act, 1948, and makes further provision with respect to the duties of education authorities in Scotland as to dental treatment. It contains 20 Sections and two Schedules.

Section 1 amends the definition of 'displaced pupils' in Section 104 (2) (a) of the 1944 Act so as to include pupils who were attending or would, in the Minister's opinion, have attended an existing voluntary aided or special agreement school, but cannot now attend that school because, owing to action taken, or proposed to be taken, under housing or town and country planning Acts, they have ceased to reside in the area served by the school.

Section 2 extends the powers given to local education authorities by Section 1 of the 1946 Act to pay for the enlargement of a voluntary controlled school, by enabling them to provide (if preferable) a wholly new school.

Section 3 relaxes (in respect of secondary schools only) the requirement that any enlargement of a voluntary controlled school under Section 1 of the 1946 Act must be conditional upon a reduction of voluntary school accommodation elsewhere.

Section 4 makes it clear that local education authorities in England and Wales have a statutory duty to make available for pupils in maintained schools and county colleges comprehensive facilities for free dental treatment. These may be provided either by persons employed and paid by the L.E.A., or under arrangements made by a Regional Hospital Board or the Board of Governors of a teaching hospital within the meaning of the National Health Service Act, 1946.

Section 5 lays an identical duty upon the education authorities in Scotland.

Section 6 makes it quite clear that local education authorities have, and are deemed always to have had, the power to make (with the Minister's approval) arrangements for the provision of primary and secondary education for pupils at non-maintained schools. For places put at their disposal by proprietors, and eligible for grant, or places taken up because of shortage of maintained school places, the L.E.A. must pay the whole of the fees. They must pay the boarding as well as the tuition fee if suitable education for a pupil cannot be provided otherwise than by boarding.

Section 7 gives local education authorities power in certain conditions to recover the cost, or part of it, of providing Further Education for pupils who do not belong to their area.

This is a detailed and intricate Section containing seven subsections. Refer to the Local Education Authorities Recoupment (Further Education) Regulations, 1954 (No. 815).

Section 8 modifies the procedure laid down in Sections 103–105 for the making of grants and loans by the Minister to managers or governors of voluntary schools. The principal change is that grants, or loans, may now be made when an existing building is purchased to provide premises for a transferred or substituted school, or for one for displaced pupils.

Section 9 makes it clear that Section 85 (3) of the 1944 Act, which states that a primary or secondary school vested in a local education authority as trustees shall be a county school, applies only to schools so vested after 1 April 1945, when the main bulk of the Education Act, 1944, came into operation.

Section 10 speeds up the procedure for making school attendance orders. A parent who has not satisfied the authority that his child is receiving efficient full-time education, and wishes to select a school for him, has now only 14 days in which to make a choice.

Section 11 enables local education authorities to bring a persistently truant child before a juvenile court, either instead of, or in addition to, bringing the parents before a magistrates' court.

Section 12 empowers local education authorities to fill vacant places in motor vehicles provided for the free transport of pupils with other pupils whom they charge reasonable fares.

Section 13 enables teachers and other persons employed in educational establishments maintained or assisted by a local education authority to be appointed as members of Children's Committees set up by local authorities under the Children Act, 1948.

Section 14 enables the Minister, on the application of the Trustees, to require that schools held on general trusts which include educational trusts shall not be diverted from educational use so long as they are required as maintained schools.

Section 15 removes the obligation, imposed by Section 87 (2) of the Education Act, 1944, on universities, colleges of a university, university colleges, and local education authorities, to send to the Minister assurances of land or personal estate (or copies thereof) to be laid out in purchases of land for educational purposes.

Section 16 reduces from three to two months the period during which objections may be submitted to the Minister about proposals for the establishment or discontinuance of a county or voluntary school.

Section 17 provides that the provisions of the 1944 and 1948

Acts shall have effect subject to the amendments and repeals specified in the First Schedule.

Section 18 provides that Regulations made under this Act shall be made in normal fashion.

Section 19 provides similarly for any increase in expenditure due to the Act.

Section 20 gives the citation of the Act, and states that Sections 5 and 19 only extend to Scotland, and no Sections to Northern Ireland.

The First Schedule lists the amendments made to the 1944 and 1948 Acts, and the Second Schedule the repeals.

The Education Act, 1959

THIS Act received the Royal Assent on 29 July 1959. It enlarges the powers of the Minister of Education to make contributions, grants and loans in respect of aided and special agreement schools. It contains two Sections only.

Section 1 (1) substitutes grants of 75 per cent. for the grants of 50 per cent. formerly payable under Section 102 of the Education Act, 1944, towards the cost of alterations and external repairs, and under Sections 103 and 104 towards the cost of building schools which are transferred or substituted schools, or are required to accommodate displaced pupils.

Subsections 2, 3, and 4 of Section 1 empower the Minister to pay grants and make loans towards the cost of providing sites or school buildings for new aided schools which are needed to give secondary education to children from aided or special agreement primary schools in the same area; these primary schools must have been established before 'the relevant date' (15 June, 1959), or approved for establishment before that day, or be schools specifically to replace such schools. Sub-section 5 defines 'replacement'.

Sub-sections 7 and 8 exclude from the benefits of the Act expenditure on work begun or approved by the Minister before 'the relevant date', or work that did not require the Minister's approval. Expenditure on sites or the purchase of existing buildings falling under either of these two heads is also excluded.

Section 2 gives the short title of the Act, and states that the Act does not extend to Scotland or Northern Ireland.

The Education Act, 1962

THIS Act received the Royal Assent on 29 March, 1962. It is un-
usual in that considerable parts of it (four sections) apply to Scotland but not to England and Wales. It makes further provision
with respect to awards and grants by local education authorities
and the Minister of Education in England and Wales, and by education authorities and the Secretary of State in Scotland; enables
the General Grant Order, 1960, and the General Grant (Scotland)
Order, 1960, to be varied to take account of resultant additional
or reduced expenditure; and it reduces the number of school
leaving dates from three to two a year. It contains 14 Sections and
two Schedules.

Section 1 lays a duty on L.E.As. in England and Wales to
bestow awards on persons ordinarily resident in their areas, and
possessing the requisite educational qualifications, in respect of
attendance at first degree or comparable courses in the United
Kingdom.

Section 2 empowers the L.E.As. to bestow awards on persons over compulsory school age, not undergoing training as
teachers, in respect of attendance at any full-time or part-time
courses of further education, in Britain or elsewhere, except those
covered by Section 1.

These changes took effect from 1 September 1962.

Section 3 authorizes the Minister to pay grants to or in respect
of persons being trained as teachers, and to bestow awards
on persons attending post-graduate or comparable courses,
and mature students attending first degree or comparable
courses.

Sections 5 and 6 empower Scottish education authorities and
the Secretary of State for Scotland to make awards to persons
over school age in attendance at full- or part-time courses of
further education.

Sections 7 and 8 empower the Minister of Housing and Local
Government to vary the provisions of the General Grant Orders
of 1960.

Section 9 states that a pupil who attains the upper limit of
compulsory school age between the beginning of September and
the end of January shall be deemed not to have attained that age

until the end of the Spring term. Section 10 makes similar provision for Scotland. These changes took effect from 1 September
1963.

Sections 11–14 contain the routine supplementary provisions: finance, interpretation, repeals, citation.

The First Schedule defines 'Ordinary Residence'.

Remuneration of Teachers Act, 1963

THIS Act, dated 10 July 1963, empowered the Minister of
Education to make provision, by Order, otherwise than in
accordance with Section 89 of the Education Act, 1944, for the
remuneration of teachers. No Order, except one revoking a
previous Order, might be made after 31 March 1965. The Act
affected teachers in maintained primary and secondary schools,
further education establishments, and farm institutes in England
and Wales. No teacher's salary was to be reduced by any Order.

The Education Act, 1964

THIS Act received the Royal Assent on 31 July 1964. Like the
1962 Act it contains provisions affecting Scotland. Section 1,
which relates only to England and Wales, enables county and
voluntary schools to be established for providing full-time education by reference to age-limits differing from those specified in the
Education Act, 1944, as amended by the Education (Miscellaneous
Provisions) Act, 1948—that is, age-limits below the age of ten
years and six months or above the age of twelve years. Sections 2
and 3, which apply respectively to England and Wales, and Scotland, enable maintenance grants to be granted in respect of pupils
at special schools who are over compulsory school age. Section 4
specifies the financial arrangements, and Section 5 gives the citation of the Act.

Remuneration of Teachers Act, 1965

THIS Act received the Royal Assent on 23 March 1965. It established new machinery for determining the salaries to be paid to teachers by local education authorities. The most important changes made were the inclusion of representatives of the Secretary of State on the employers' panel of any negotiating committee, and the provision for resort to arbitration should negotiation fail.

The Act contains 9 clauses.

Clause 1 provides for the setting up of one or more committees to consider the remuneration payable to teachers. A committee consists of an independent chairman and of representatives of the Secretary of State and of local education authorities on the one side and of representatives of teachers on the other. The Secretary of State appoints the chairman, and determines what bodies shall represent local education authorities and teachers.

Clause 2 requires each committee to review the remuneration of teachers of the description with which it is concerned (e.g., schools or further education) and to transmit their agreed recommendations to the Secretary of State, who must then, in consultation with the committee, give effect to them.

Clause 3 enables matters on which a committee has been unable to reach agreement to be referred to arbitration.

Clause 4 required that effect be given to the arbitrators' recommendations unless each House of Parliament resolves that national and economic circumstances require that this shall not happen. In such case the Secretary of State is authorized to determine, in consultation with the committee concerned, what changes (if any) are appropriate.

Clauses 5–9 contain supplementary and financial provisions.

The machinery set up by this Act applies only to England and Wales, except that Section 6 (financial provisions) is applicable also to Scotland.

The Education Act, 1967

THIS Act received the Royal Assent on 16 February 1967. It enlarges the powers of the Secretary of State for Education and Science to make contributions, grants and loans in respect of aided and special agreement schools, and to direct L.E.As. to pay the expenses of establishing or enlarging controlled schools; and to provide for loans for capital expenditure incurred for purposes of colleges of education by persons other than L.E.As. It contains 6 Sections.

Section 1 empowers the Secretary of State to make contributions equal to or grants not exceeding 80 per cent. (in place of the 75 per cent. of the 1959 Act) of certain expenses incurred in the maintenance or provision of aided and special agreement schools.

Section 2 includes primary as well as secondary schools among those controlled schools whose enlargement shall be paid for by the L.E.A.

Section 3 extends the Secretary of State's power so as to require L.E.As. to defray the expenses of establishing a controlled 'middle school'.

Section 4 empowers the Secretary of State to make provision by regulations for his making loans out of Parliamentary moneys to persons other than L.E.As. in aid of capital expenditure for providing, replacing, extending, improving, furnishing or equipping colleges of education.

Sections 5 and 6 are routine: finance and citation. The Act affects England and Wales only.

The Education (Scotland) Act, 1945

THE system of public education in Scotland is quite distinct from that of England and Wales, and separate Acts of Parliament are required to reform or amend it.

The Education (Scotland) Act, 1945, was 'an Act to *amend* the law relating to education in Scotland'; not, it will be noted, an Act to *reform* the law, as was the Education Act, 1944. No major reconstruction of the Scottish system was required, because this was already organized in progressive stages. Nor was there any 'Dual System' in Scotland: consequently, no elaborate compromise with the religious denominations had to be agreed. The purpose of the Act was to bring the Scottish system into line with the general policy of the British Government for education in Great Britain. The Act was the following year incorporated into the Education (Scotland) Act, 1946, which consolidated the law, and in 1962, along with Acts passed after 1946, in another consolidating Act, the Education (Scotland) Act, 1962.

The 1945 Act, which received the Royal Assent on 15 June 1945, is in five parts, containing 89 sections and 6 schedules.

Part I (Sections 1–19) deals with the provision of education by the local education authorities,[1] Part II (Sections 20–43) with the rights and duties of parents and the functions of education authorities in relation to individual pupils, Part III (Sections 44–65) with administration and staffing, Part IV (Sections 66–71) with independent schools, Part V (Sections 72–89) with a variety of miscellaneous matters.

Part IV is identical with Part III in the Education Act, 1944, except that the Minister concerned is the Secretary of State for

---

[1] Of which there are 35; four large burghs and 31 counties. The word 'local' is inserted here for the sake of clarity; in Scotland, the term used is 'education authorities'.

Scotland, and that it provides (Section 69) that any person disqualified from being a proprietor of an independent school or a
teacher in any school under the Education Act, 1944, is also disqualified in Scotland.

Many sections in Parts I, II, III, and V are similarly identical in intent with sections in the English Act, though as a rule they
are not worded in precisely the same form.

Among these sections are:

PART I

Section 1. Duty of education authorities to provide efficient
education throughout the three stages of primary, secondary, and
further education.

Section 3. Duty of the authorities to provide facilities for
recreation and social and physical training.

Section 7. The Secretary of State to make regulations prescribing the categories of handicapped children for whom the
authorities must secure special educational treatment.

Section 13. Standards for school buildings.

PART II

Section 20. Pupils to be educated in accordance with the
wishes of the parents.

Section 22. Duty of the parent.

Section 23. Compulsory school age.

Section 29. Further education in 'Junior Colleges' (the
equivalent of the English 'County Colleges').

Section 32. Provision (by scholarship and other benefits) to
enable pupils to take advantage of educational facilities.

Section 34. Provision of transport and other facilities.

Section 36. Provision of milk and meals at schools and junior
colleges.

Section 38. Provision of medical inspection and treatment.

Sections 40–41. Duty of the education authorities to ascertain
children suffering from mental or physical disability, and to secure
special educational treatment where necessary.

Section 51. Removal of bar against married women teachers.

Section 78. Power to education authorities to provide for
the conduct or assistance of research.

The above examples are illustrative only, and must not be

taken as an exhaustive list. Further, sections consequential upon the above (e.g. Sections 25–28, dealing with the failure of a parent to fulfil the duty laid upon him by Section 22) are likewise similar to the corresponding sections in the English Act.

The definitions of primary education and secondary education in Section 1 provide an interesting comparison with the definitions in Section 8 of the English Act.

'Primary education' means progressive elementary education in such subjects as may be prescribed in the code,[1] regard being had to the age, ability, and aptitude of the pupils concerned, and such education shall be given in primary schools or departments. Primary education includes training by appropriate methods in schools and classes (hereinafter referred to as 'nursery schools' and 'nursery classes') for pupils between the age of two years and such later age as may be permitted by the code.

'Secondary education' means progressive courses of instruction of such length and in such subjects as may be approved in terms of the code as appropriate to the age, ability, and aptitude of the pupils who have been promoted from primary schools and departments and to the period for which they may be expected to remain at school. Such courses shall be given in secondary schools or departments.

It will be noted how much more full and precise are the Scottish definitions. Another interesting comparison is found (Section 1) in respect of nursery education.

The provision of primary education in nursery schools and nursery classes shall be deemed to be adequate if such provision is made at centres where sufficient children whose parents desire such education for them can be enrolled to form a school or class of a reasonable size.

Here the onus of proving the demand appears to be laid on the parents, whereas in the English Act it is laid on the Minister and the local education authority.

In respect of secondary education, the 1945 Act[2] laid down that—

---

[1] The regulations made by the Secretary of State 'may include codes relating to the conduct of schools, junior colleges, and other educational establishments, and the education to be provided therein' (Section 55). In the 1962 Act the word 'regulations' replaces 'codes'.

[2] In the 1962 Act all the words after 'profiting' are omitted.

The provision of secondary education shall be deemed to be adequate if a reasonable variety of courses is provided, from which the parent of a pupil may select a course from which, in the opinion of the education authority, the pupil shows reasonable promise of profiting, and the parent shall not be entitled to select a course of secondary education from which, in the opinion of the education authority (confirmed by the Secretary of State in the event of a dispute between the parent and the authority), the pupil shows no reasonable promise of profiting.

Here the Scottish definition appears to be somewhat narrower than the English, in that it does not offer so wide a choice of courses. But again it appears to throw more responsibility for choice on the parent.

In England and Wales no tuition fees may be charged in maintained primary and secondary schools. This is not the case in Scotland. Section 11 of the 1945 Act reads—

Primary, secondary, and compulsory further education provided in public schools[1] and junior colleges under the management of an education authority shall be without payment of fees, provided that if the authority think it expedient they may charge fees in some or all of the classes in a limited number of primary[2] and secondary schools, provided further that the power to charge fees may be exercised without prejudice to the adequate provision of free primary and secondary education. . .

In England and Wales fees in elementary schools were almost completely eliminated in 1891, and finally abolished in 1918. Fees in maintained secondary schools were abolished by the 1944 Act.

Local administration of education is somewhat differently organized in Scotland. The following are among the salient points.

1   The authority is the council of a county or a large burgh. There are no divisional executives.

2   The authority may, and must if so required by the Secretary

---

[1] A 'public school' in Scotland is literally 'a school for the public'. It is defined in Section 87 as 'any school under the management of an education authority'.

[2] There are cases where in the same school tuition fees are payable in the primary but not the secondary department.

of State, submit a scheme for the constitution of an education committee.[1]

3   Every scheme must provide for the delegation of the functions of the council relating to education to the education committee: except that—

A   *The following powers may not be delegated:*

i   The raising of money by rate or loan;

ii   The approval of the estimates (including supplementary estimates) of capital and revenue expenditure and the authorization of the expenditure included therein;

iii   The power to incur expenditure on behalf of the council other than expenditure previously authorized in estimates or expenditure necessarily incurred in circumstances of urgency.

B   *The following powers may be excluded from the delegation to the education committee:*

i   Acquisition and disposal of land;

ii   Appointment, dismissal, remuneration, and conditions of service (except functions) of the director of education and of any deputy or assistant director of education;

iii   Remuneration and conditions of service of staff other than teachers;

iv   The school health service;

v   Any other function which the council satisfy the Secretary of State should not be delegated (Section 44).

4   The provision of public education by an education authority is to be in accordance with a scheme approved by the Secretary of State.

5   Public education in Scotland, as in England, is financed partly from the Exchequer and partly from local rates, with some small revenue coming from fees. Most of the Exchequer share is provided through General Grants paid to local authorities through the Scottish Development Department. But the Scottish Education Department pays grants to some voluntary schools and colleges, and meets the cost of the inspection

[1] This provision, and the whole of the matter listed under (3), are omitted from the 1962. Act.

of schools and of the Scottish Certificate of Education examination.

The responsibility of the Minister for the training of teachers is more direct than in England. Section 49 lays down that—

The Secretary of State may by regulations constitute, alter the constitution of, incorporate and dissolve committees or other bodies for the training of teachers . . . and may prescribe the duties to be formed by the said committees . . . including the courses of training to be provided. . . .

and

. . . May award certificates of competency to teach, and . . . by regulations prescribe the forms of the said certificates, the conditions of award and the conditions under which they may be withdrawn. . . .

By the same section the National Committee for the Training of Teachers, and the Provincial Committees and committees of management deriving from it,[1] are deemed to be committees constituted under the Act.

There is no 'Burnham Committee' in Scotland. By Section 50 it is the duty of every education authority—

To pay to the teachers appointed by them salaries in accordance with such scales as may from time to time be prescribed by regulations made by the Secretary of State.

An interesting item not found in the English Act is that—

The Secretary of State shall appoint one of his officers to be Registrar of Educational Endowments, and it shall be the duty of the Registrar to keep a register of all educational endowments, which . . . shall be open to public inspection at all reasonable times.

It will be seen that in general, central control and direction is stronger in Scotland than in England and Wales.

---

[1] The Provincial committees were replaced in 1959 by the Governing Bodies of the Colleges of Education (training colleges) and the National Committee by an advisory and co-ordinating Scottish Council for the Training of Teachers with a membership built up from the Governing Bodies. In 1966 there was established, by Act of Parliament passed in 1965, a General Teaching Council with wide functions in respect of teachers and their training. It took over the work of the Scottish Council.